The New Modern Roc

BIG BOOK

Project Manager: Aaron Stang
Cover Design: Joann Carrera

Contents

Artist Index

ALL YOU WANTED

All gtrs. Capo I

Words and Music by
MICHELLE BRANCH

Verse 3:
I'm sinking slowly,
So hurry hold me,
Your hand is all I have to keep me hanging on.
Please can you tell me,
So I can finally see
Where you go when you're gone.
(To Chorus:)

AMERICAN IDIOT

Words by BILLIE JOE
Music by GREEN DAY

14

American Idiot - 7 - 3

Verse 3:
w/Rhy. Fig. 1 *(Elec. Gtr. 1)*

Don't want to be an A - mer - i - can id - i - ot, one na - tion con - trolled

18

we're not the ones___ who're meant to fol - low,___

___ for that's e - nough___ to ar - gue.

Outro:

Elec. Gtr. 1

Elec. Gtr. 2 enters

Elec. Gtr. 1

Elec. Gtr. 2 enters

BRIAN WILSON

Words and Music by
STEVEN PAGE

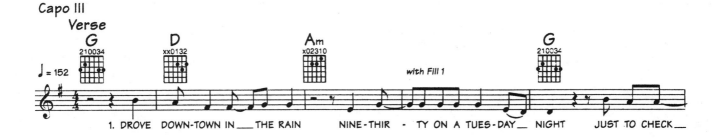

1. DROVE DOWN-TOWN IN THE RAIN NINE-THIR-TY ON A TUES-DAY NIGHT JUST TO CHECK

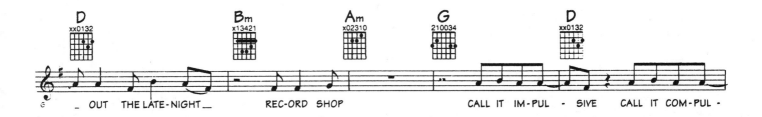

OUT THE LATE-NIGHT REC-ORD SHOP CALL IT IM-PUL-SIVE CALL IT COM-PUL-

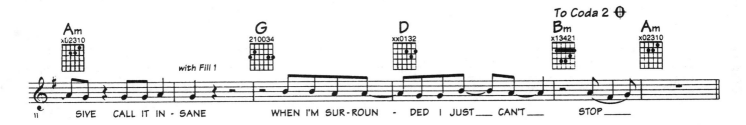

SIVE CALL IT IN-SANE WHEN I'M SUR-ROUN-DED I JUST CAN'T STOP

2. IT'S A MAT-TER OF IN-STINCT IT'S A MAT-TER OF CON-DI-TION-ING AND A MAT-TER OF FACT
3. See additional lyrics.

YOU CAN CALL ME PAV-LOV'S DOG RING A BELL

Fill 1

Brian Wilson - 3 - 1

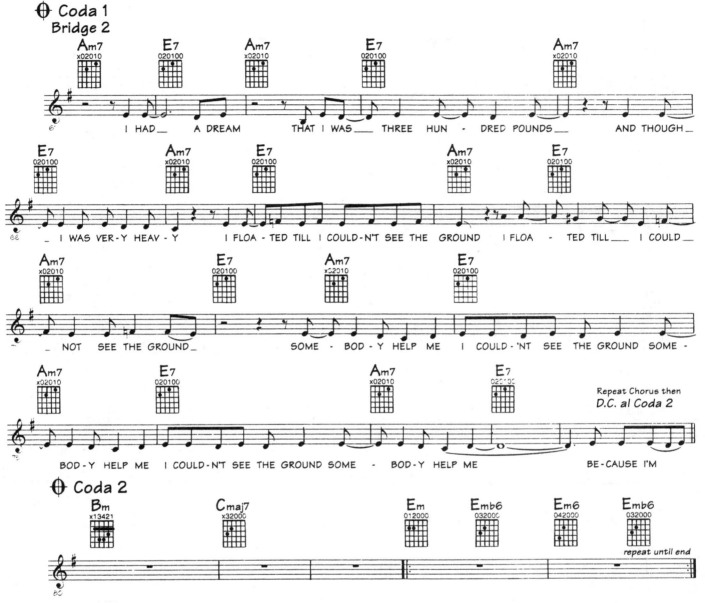

1. DROVE DOWNTOWN IN THE RAIN
NINE-THIRTY ON A TUESDAY NIGHT
JUST TO CHECK OUT THE LATE-NIGHT RECORD SHOP
CALL IT IMPULSIVE, CALL IT COMPULSIVE, CALL IT INSANE
WHEN I'M SURROUNDED I JUST CAN'T STOP

2. IT'S A MATTER OF INSTINCT
IT'S A MATTER OF CONDITIONING AND A MATTER OF FACT
YOU CAN CALL ME PAVLOV'S DOG
RING A BELL AND I'LL SALIVATE, HOW'D YOU LIKE THAT
DR. LANDY TELL ME YOU'RE NOT JUST A PEDAGOGUE
'CAUSE RIGHT NOW I'M

    LYING IN BED JUST LIKE BRIAN WILSON DID
    WELL I'M LYING IN BED JUST LIKE BRIAN WILSON DID

3. SO I'M LYING HERE JUST STARING AT THE CEILING TILES
AND I'M THINKING ABOUT WHAT TO THINK ABOUT
JUST LISTENING AND RELISTENING TO *SMILEY SMILE*
AND I'M WONDERING IF THIS IS SOME KIND OF
CREATIVE DROUGHT BECAUSE I'M

    CHORUS

Bridge 1
AND IF YOU WANT TO FIND ME I'LL BE
OUT IN THE SANDBOX
JUST WONDERING A WHERE THE HELL
ALL THE LOVE HAS GONE
PLAYING MY GUITAR AND BUILDING
CASTLES IN THE SUN
AND SINGING "FUN FUN FUN"

    CHORUS

Bridge 2
I HAD A DREAM THAT I WAS THREE HUNDRED POUNDS
AND THOUGH I WAS VERY HEAVY
I FLOATED TILL I COULDN'T SEE THE GROUND
I FLOATED TILL I COULD NOT SEE THE GROUND
SOMEBODY HELP ME, I COULDN'T SEE THE GROUND
SOMEBODY HELP ME, I COULDN'T SEE THE GROUND
SOMEBODY HELP ME, BECAUSE I'M

    CHORUS

Repeat Verse 1

Brian Wilson - 3 - 3

BASKET CASE

Words by
BILLIE JOE

Music by
BILLIE JOE,
TRÉ COOL and MIKE DIRNT

24

Some-times my mind __ plays tricks __ on _____ me.

It all keeps ad - ding up. _____ I

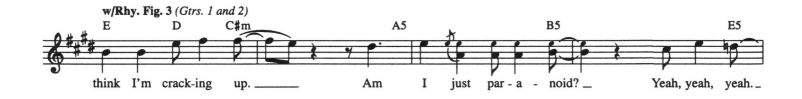

think I'm crack-ing up. _____ Am I just par - a - noid? _ Yeah, yeah, yeah. _

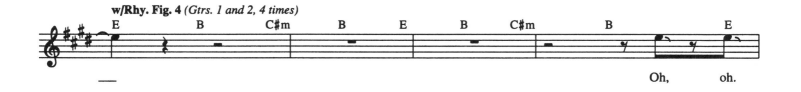

__ Oh, oh.

Grasp-

Bridge:

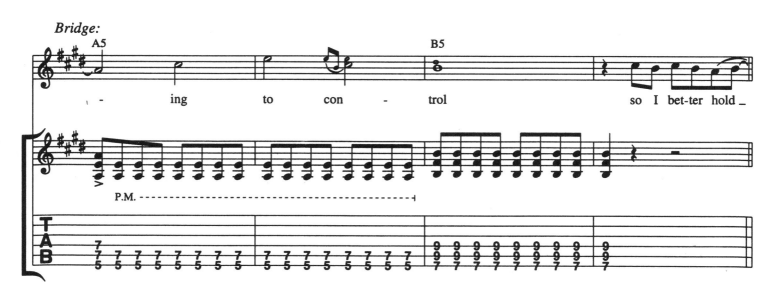

- ing to con - trol so I bet-ter hold _

P.M. --

BODIES

All gtrs. in Drop D, down 1 whole step:

⑥ = C   ③ = F
⑤ = G   ② = A
④ = C   ① = D

Music and Words by
Dave Williams, Mike Luce, C J Pierce, Stevie Benton

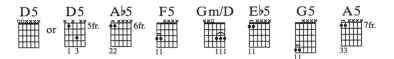

D5   D5   Ab5   F5   Gm/D   Eb5   G5   A5

Moderately ♩ = 120

Intro:
N.C.

(Whisper) *Let the bod-ies hit the floor.   Let the bod-ies hit the floor.   Let the bod-ies hit the*

*Music sounds a whole step lower than written.

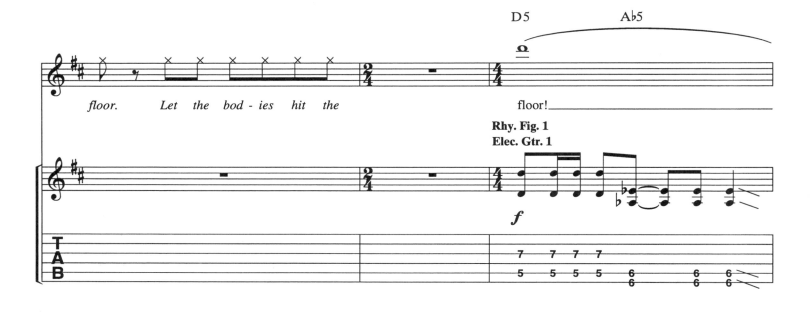

floor.   Let the bod-ies hit the   floor!_____

D5   Ab5

Rhy. Fig. 1
Elec. Gtr. 1

f

D5   Ab5   F5   D5   Ab5   D5   Ab5   F5

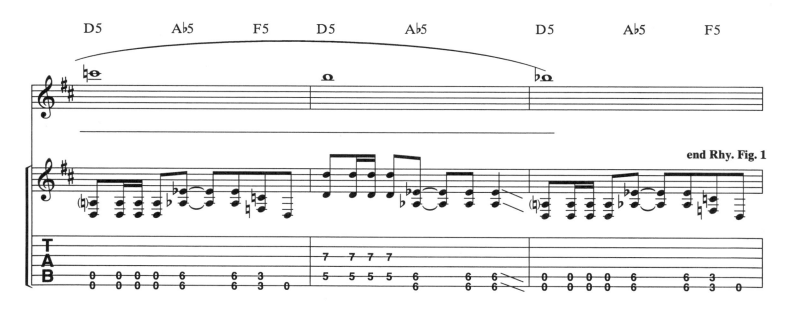

end Rhy. Fig. 1

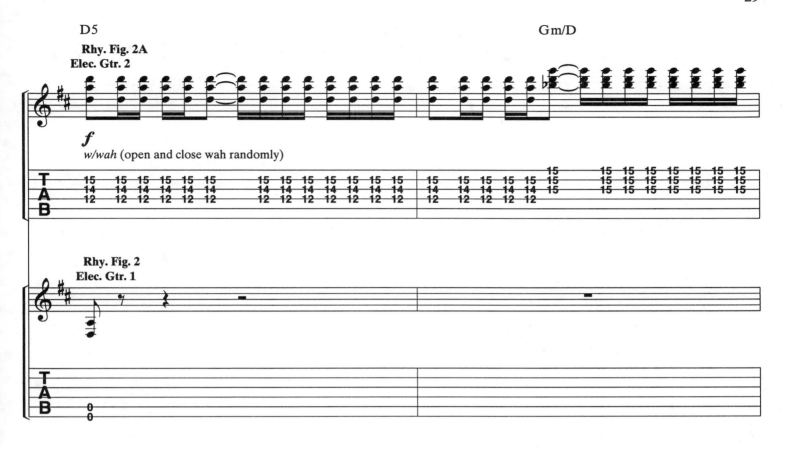

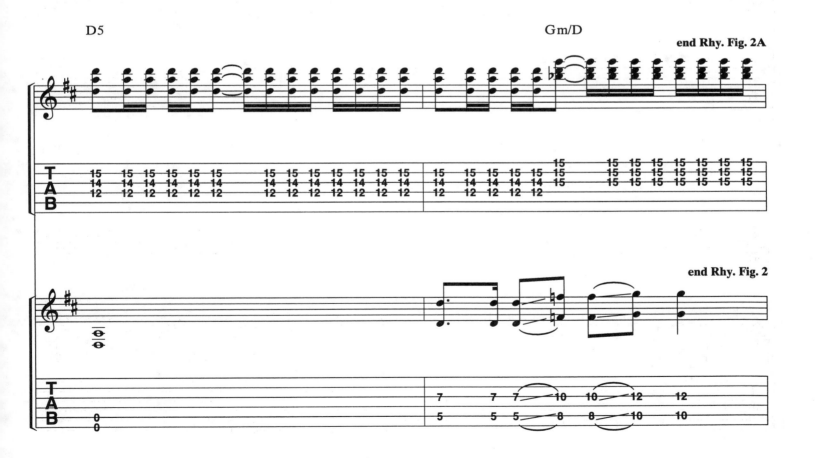

30

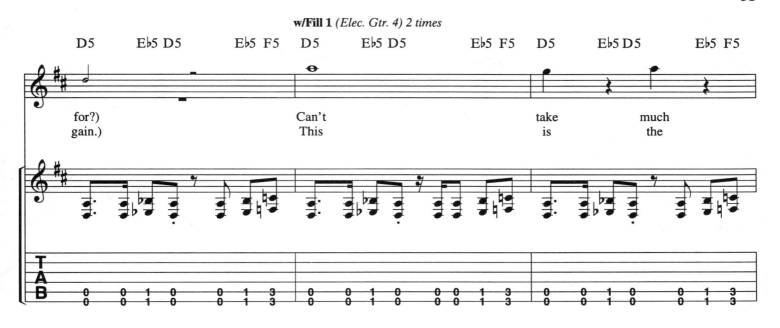

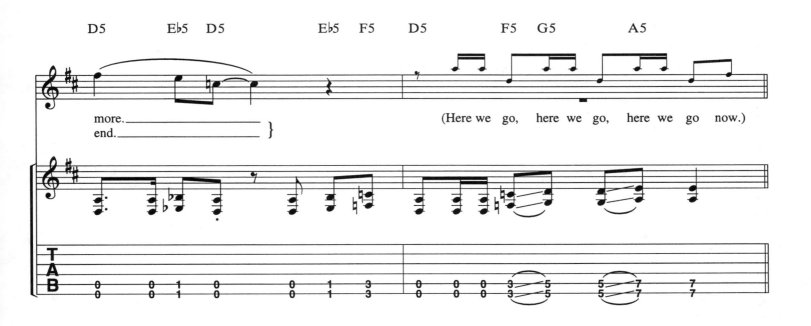

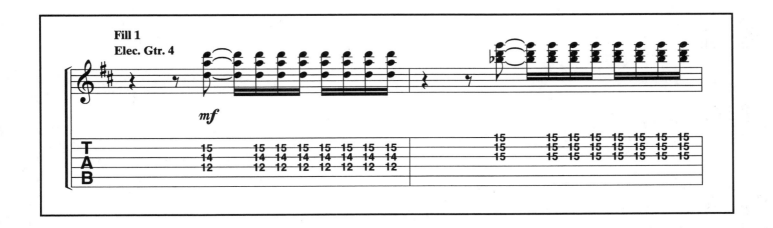

32

Pre-chorus:

Substitute w/Rhy. Fill 1 *(Elec. Gtr. 1) 3rd time only*

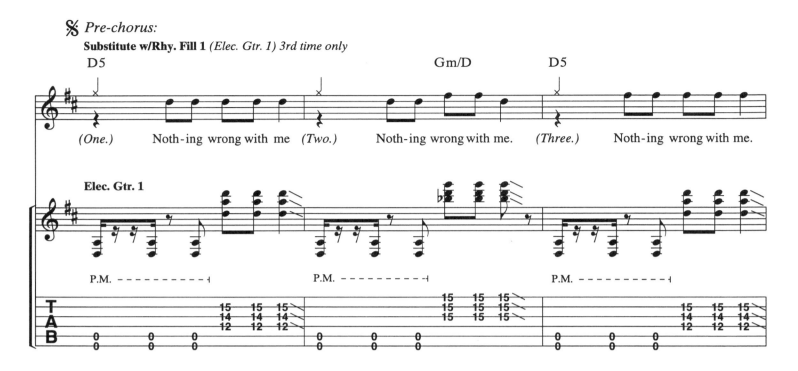

(One.) Noth-ing wrong with me (Two.) Noth-ing wrong with me. (Three.) Noth-ing wrong with me.

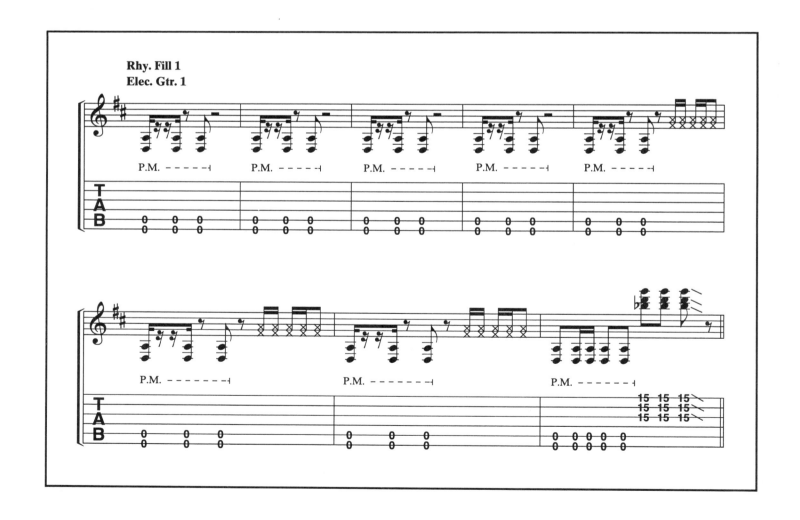

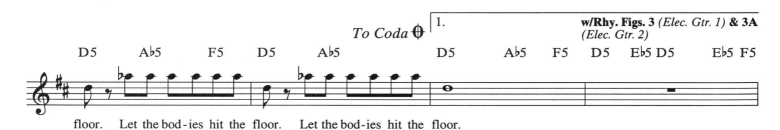

floor. Let the bod-ies hit the floor. Let the bod-ies hit the floor.

Move! floor.

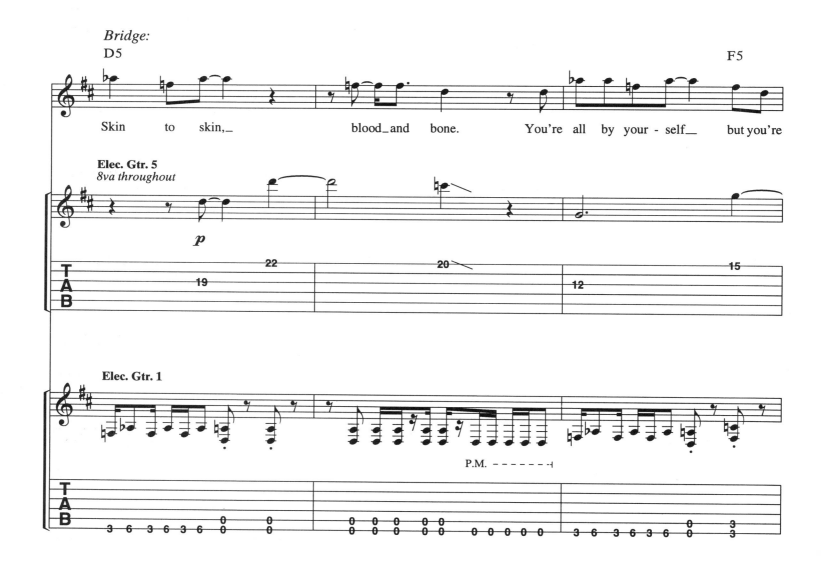

Skin to skin,_ blood_and bone. You're all by your-self_ but you're

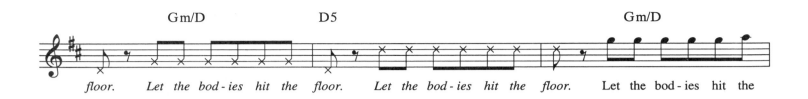

floor. Let the bod-ies hit the *floor.* Let the bod-ies hit the *floor.* Let the bod-ies hit the

w/Rhy. Figs. 3 *(Elec. Gtr. 1)* **& 3A** *(Elec. Gtr. 2)*

floor.

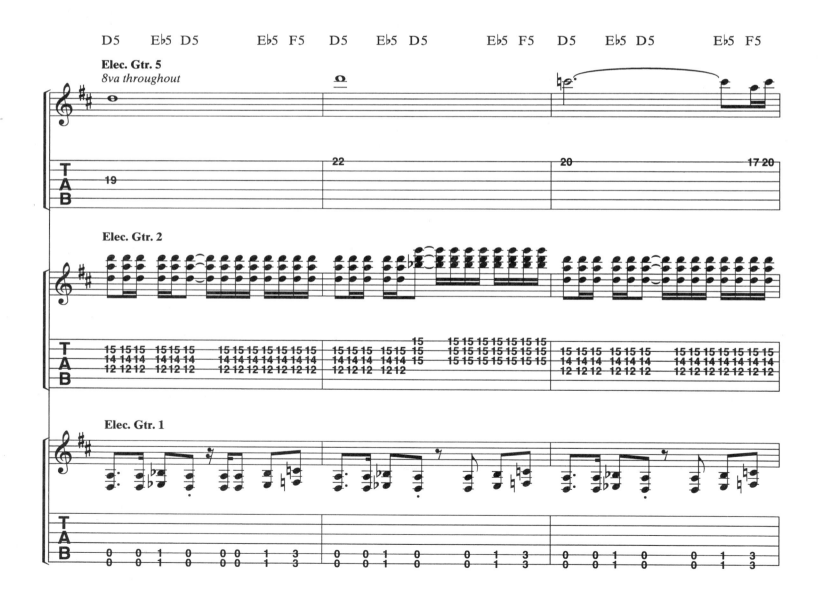

BROKEN

Words and Music by
SHAUN WELGEMOED and DALE STEWART

Slowly ♩ = 62
Intro:

Broken - 4 - 1

Guitar Solo:
w/Rhy. Figs. 1 (Acous. Gtr. 2)
& 1A (Acous. Gtr. 1) both 2 times, simile

EVERYDAY IS A WINDING ROAD

Words and Music by
SHERYL CROW, BRIAN MacLEOD and JEFF TROTT

Everyday Is a Winding Road - 8 - 1

Verses 1 & 2:
w/Rhy. Fig. 1 *(Gtr. 1) 2 times*
w/Riff A *(Gtr. 2) 2 times, Verse 2 only*

1. I hitched a ride____ with a vend - ing ma - chine re - pair - man. He says he's been__ down__ this
2. *See additional lyrics*

road more than twice.__ He__ was high__ on__ in - tel - lec - tu - al - ism.__

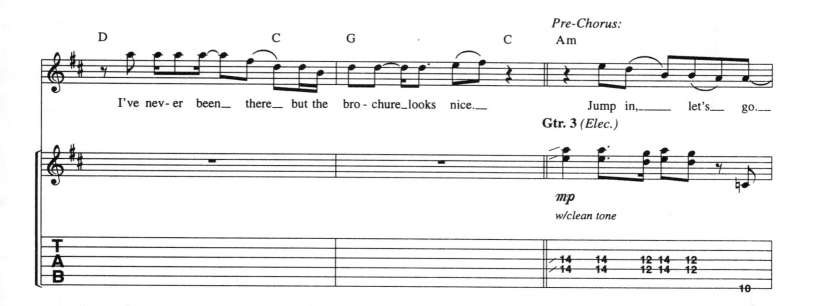

I've nev - er been__ there__ but the bro - chure__ looks nice.__ Jump in,____ let's__ go.__

Pre-Chorus:
Am

Gtr. 3 *(Elec.)*

mp
w/clean tone

Lay back,__ en - joy the show.__

44

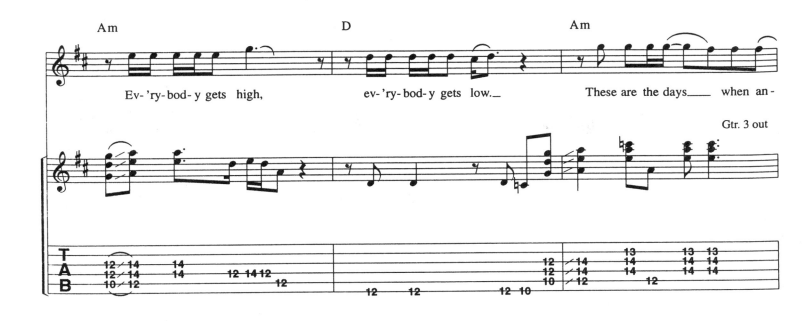

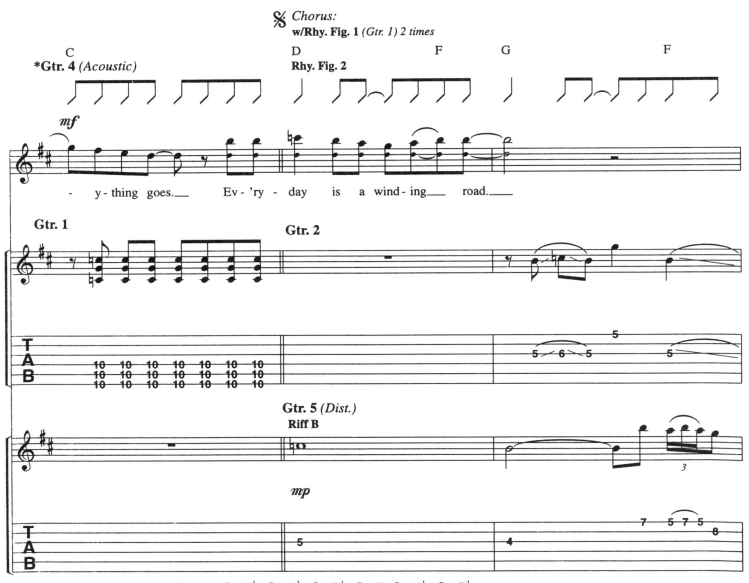

*Open D tuning, tuned down 1/2 step: ⑥ = D♭, ⑤ = A♭, ④ = D♭, ③ = F, ② = A♭, ① = D♭.

Everyday Is a Winding Road - 8 - 3

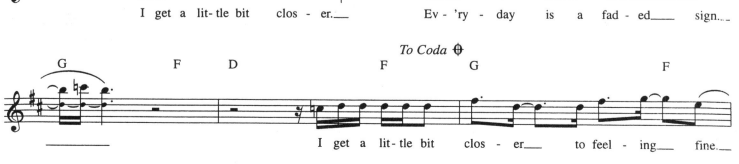

48

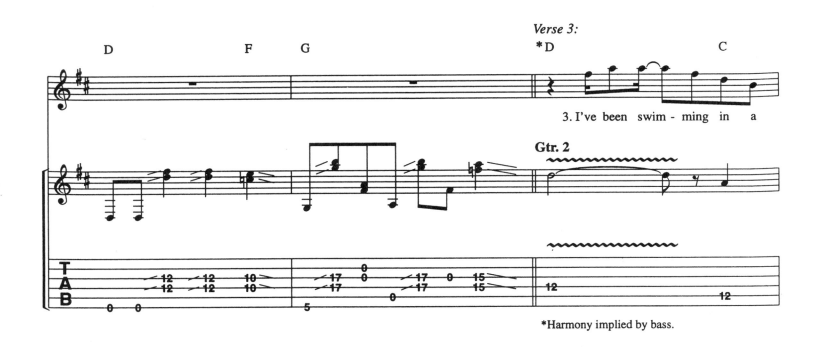

*Harmony implied by bass.

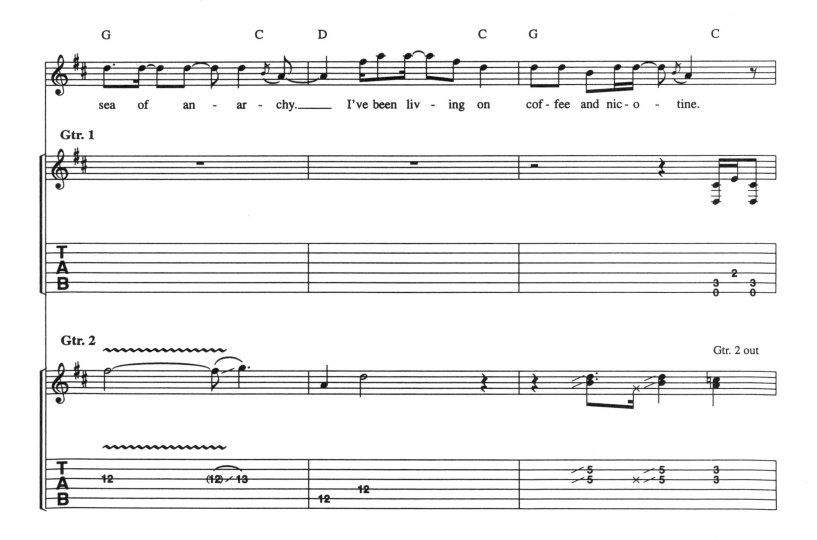

Verse 2:
He's got a daughter he calls Easter,
She was born on a Tuesday night.
I'm just wondering why I feel so all alone,
Why I'm a stranger in my own life.
(To Pre-Chorus:)

BRING ME TO LIFE

Written by Ben Moody,
Amy Lee and David Hodges

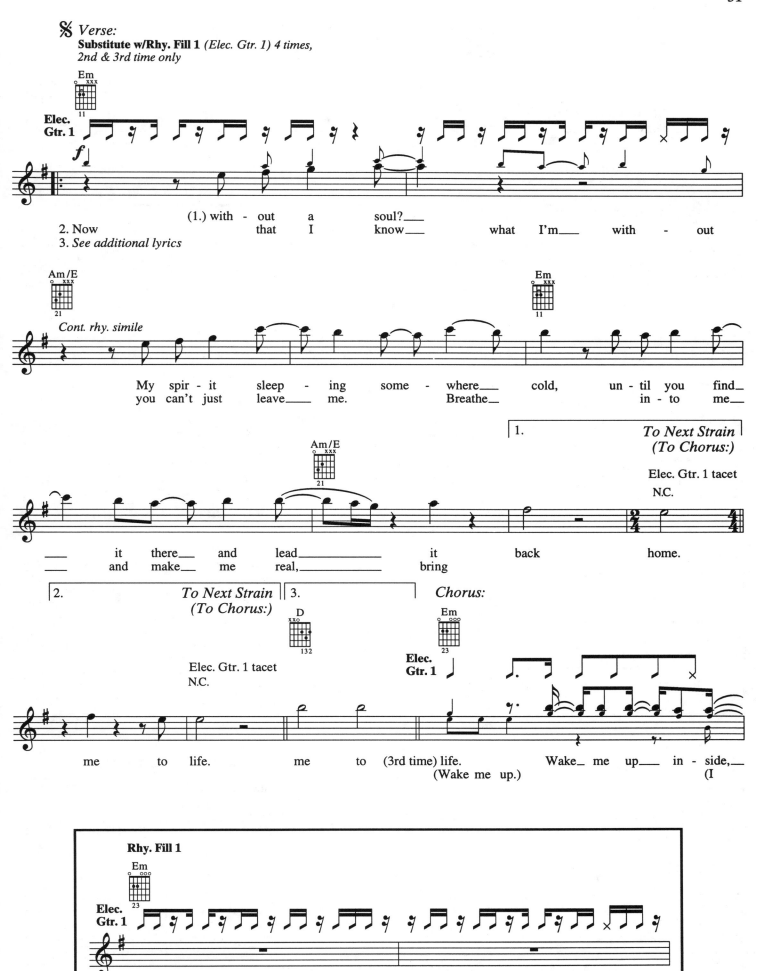

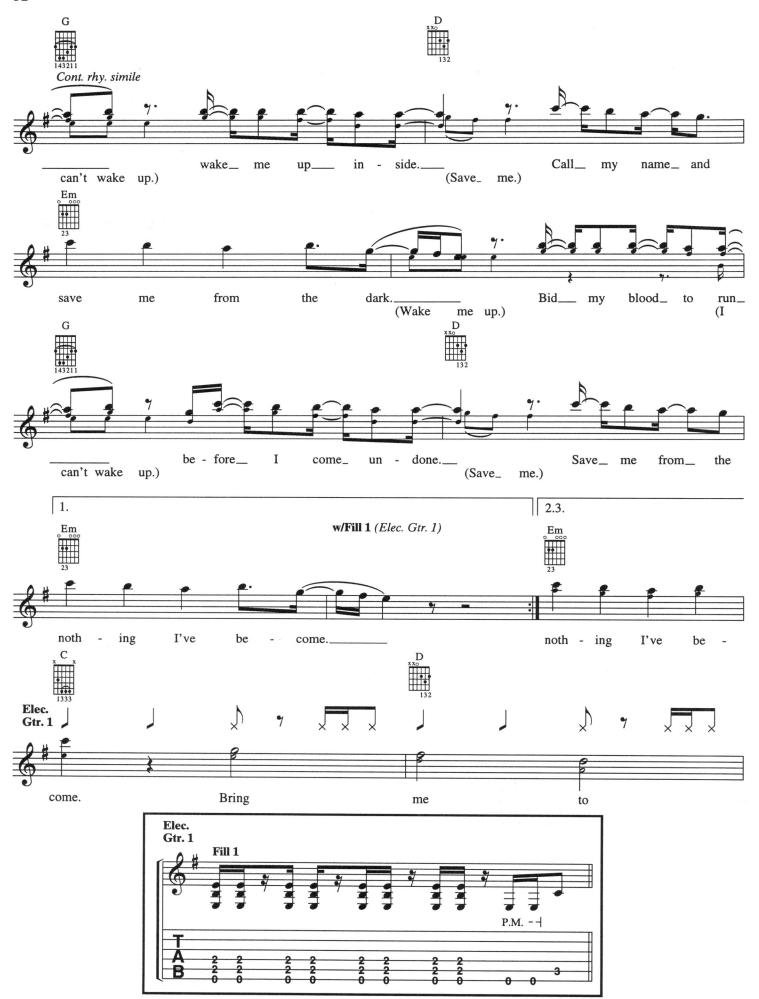

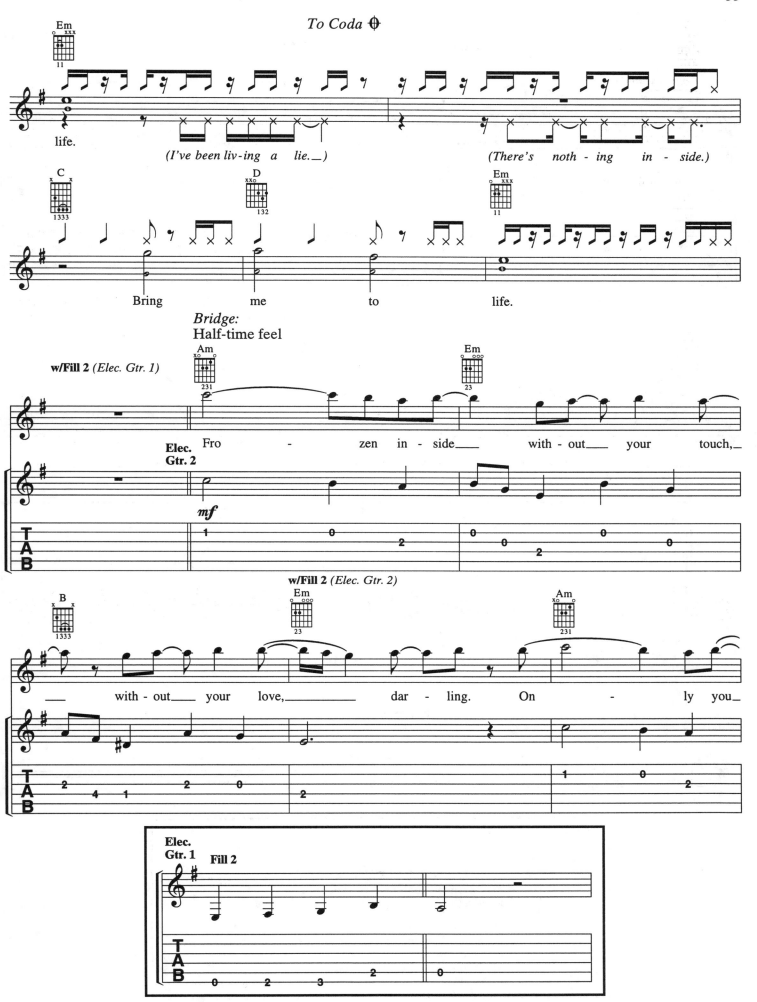

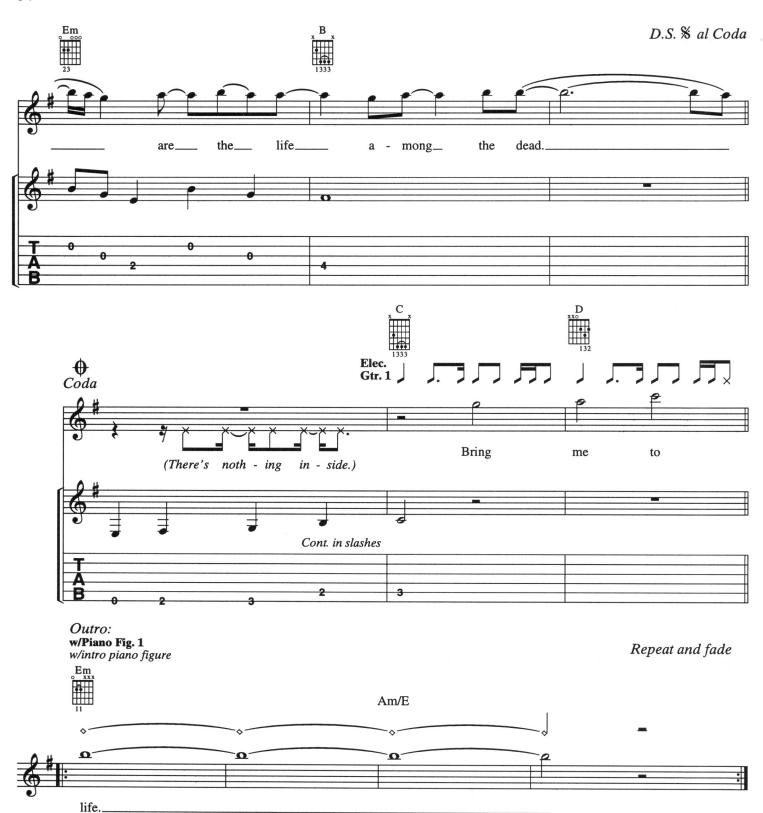

D.S. % al Coda

are the life a - mong the dead.

Coda

(There's noth - ing in - side.)

Elec. Gtr. 1

Bring me to

Cont. in slashes

Outro:
w/Piano Fig. 1
w/intro piano figure

Repeat and fade

Am/E

life.

Verse 3:
All this time I can't believe I couldn't see.
Kept in the dark, but you were there in front of me.
I've been sleeping a thousand years, it seems.
Got to open my eyes to everything.
Without a thought, without a voice, without a soul,
Don't let me die here.
There must be something more.
Bring me to life.
(To Chorus:)

CLOSING TIME

Words and Music by
DAN WILSON

Moderate rock ♩ = 92
Intro:

*Two gtrs. arranged for one.

**Piano arr. for gtr.

Verses 1 & 2:
w/Rhy. Fig. 1 *(Gtr. 1)* **& Riff A** *(Gtr. 2) Both 8 times*

1. Clos-ing time,__ o-pen all the doors_ and let____ you out in-to the world.__
2. Clos-ing time,__ time for you to go out to the plac-es you will_ be from.__

Clos-ing time,__ turn all of the lights_ on o-ver
Clos-ing time,__ this room won't be o-pen till your

ev-'ry boy and ev-er-y girl.____ Clos-ing time,__
broth-ers or your sis-ters come.__ So gath-er up your jack-ets,

Closing Time - 5 - 1

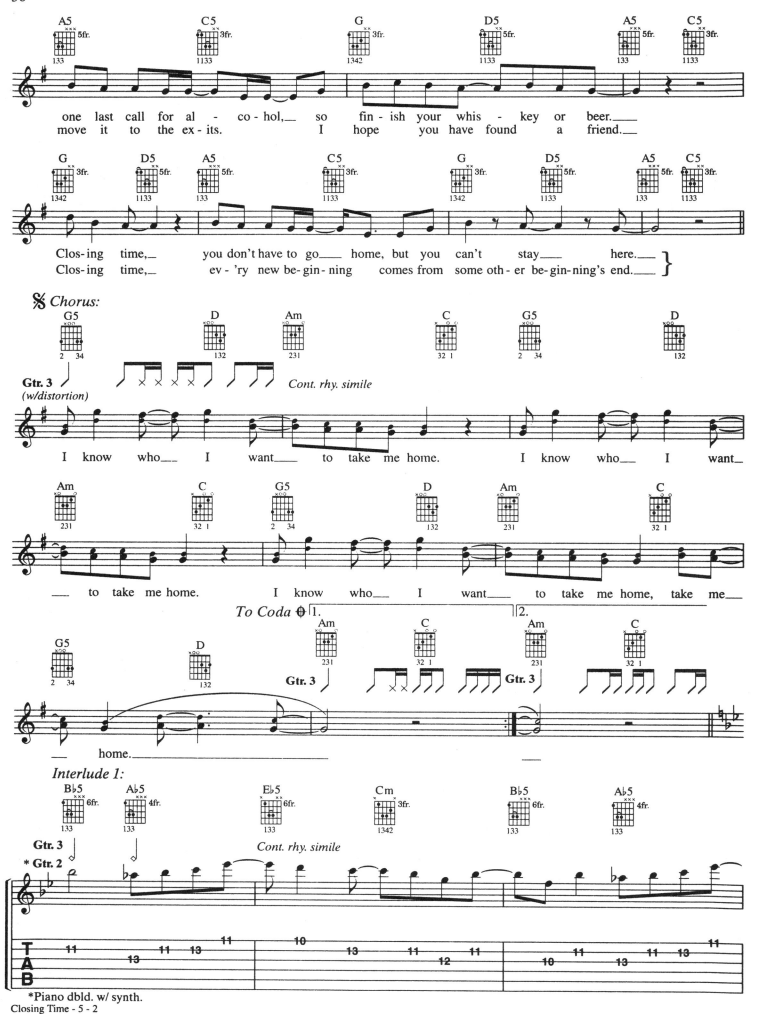

one last call for al - co - hol,_ so fin - ish your whis - key or beer.___
move it to the ex - its. I hope you have found a friend.___

Clos - ing time,_ you don't have to go__ home, but you can't stay___ here.___ }
Clos - ing time,_ ev - 'ry new be - gin - ning comes from some oth - er be - gin - ning's end.___ }

Chorus:

Gtr. 3
(w/distortion)

Cont. rhy. simile

I know who__ I want___ to take me home. I know who__ I want_

___ to take me home. I know who__ I want___ to take me home, take me___

To Coda

Gtr. 3   **Gtr. 3**

__ home.

Interlude 1:

Gtr. 3

Cont. rhy. simile

* Gtr. 2

*Piano dbld. w/ synth.

Closing Time - 5 - 2

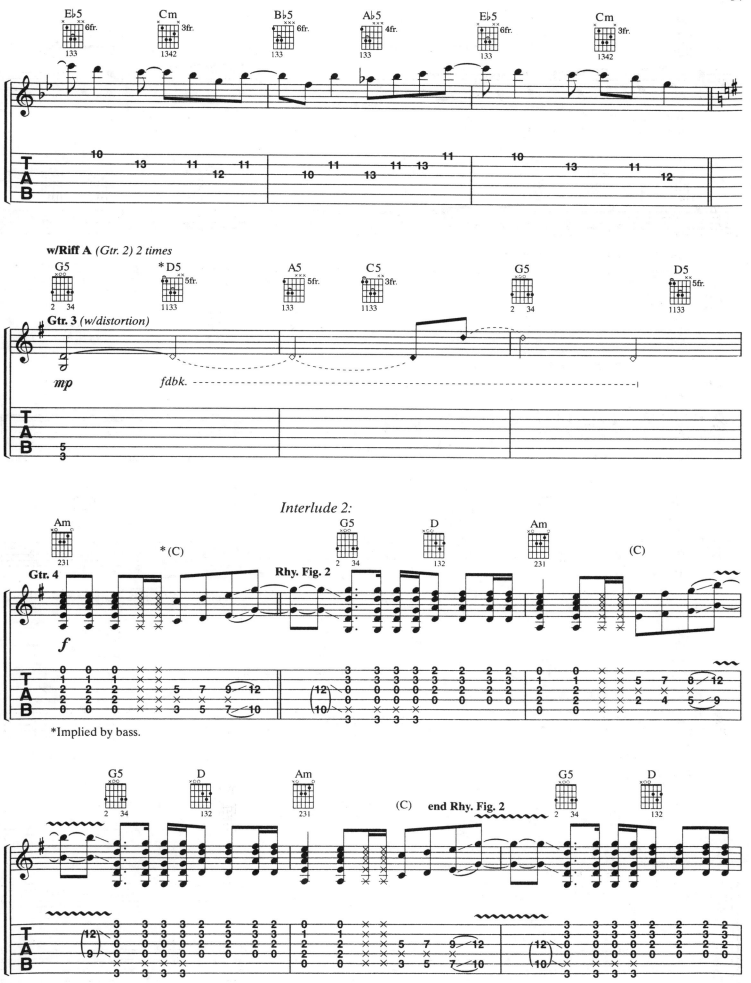

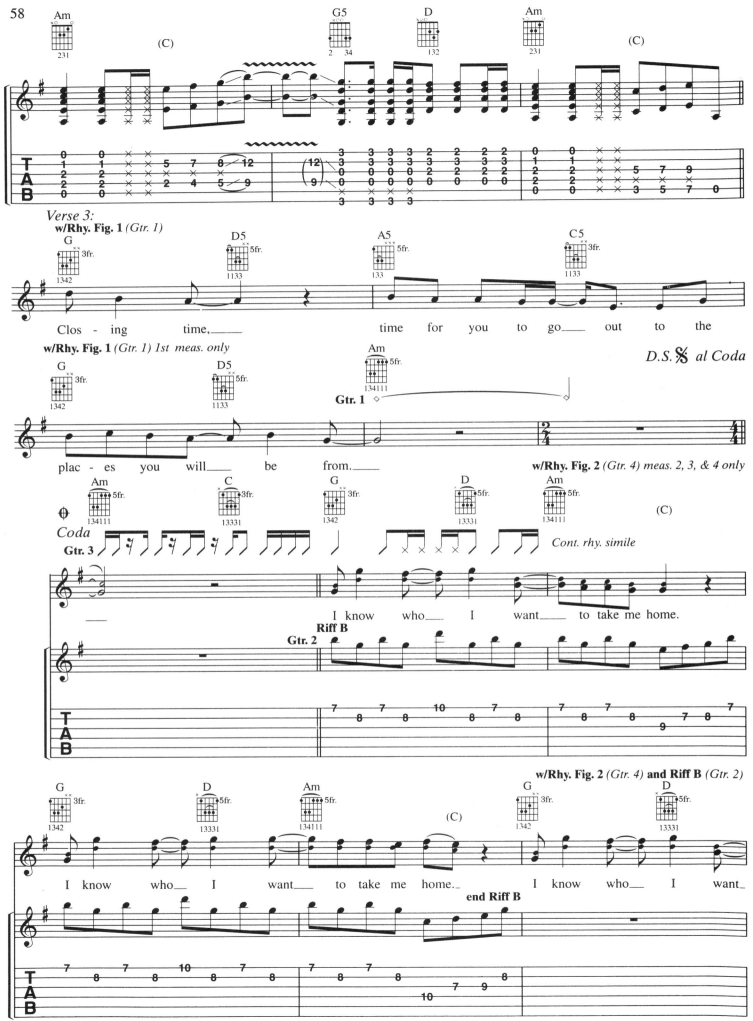

Verse 3:
w/Rhy. **Fig. 1** (*Gtr. 1*)

Clos- ing time,_____ time for you to go___ out to the

w/Rhy. **Fig. 1** (*Gtr. 1*) *1st meas. only*

D.S. 𝄋 *al Coda*

Gtr. 1

plac- es you will___ be from.____

w/Rhy. **Fig. 2** (*Gtr. 4*) *meas. 2, 3, & 4 only*

Coda
Gtr. 3

Cont. rhy. simile

I know who___ I want___ to take me home.

Riff B
Gtr. 2

w/Rhy. **Fig. 2** (*Gtr. 4*) **and Riff B** (*Gtr. 2*)

I know who___ I want___ to take me home._ I know who___ I want_

end Riff B

CRAWLING IN THE DARK

All gtrs. w/Open E tuning:
E-B-E-G#-B-E
⑥ = E   ③ = G#
⑤ = B   ② = B
④ = E   ① = E

Words and Music by
DANIEL ESTRIN and DOUGLAS ROBB

Moderate rock ♩ = 92
Intro:
N.C.
Gtr. 1 *(w/slight dist.)*

mf w/delay
P.M. throughout

Gtr. 1 tacet

E5 F#5   E5 F#5 D5   A/C#   A5   E5

Gtr. 2 *(w/dist.)*

f

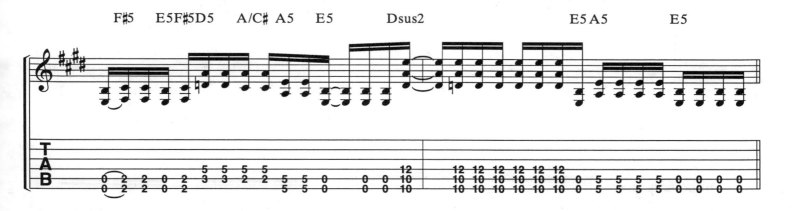

62

w/Riff A (Gtr. 1)
w/misc. feedback (next 3 meas.)
w/Riff B (Gtr. 3) 2 times, 2nd time only

And I_____ wish I could know___ of the di - rec - tions that___ I take___
Will___ the end-ing be___ ev - er com - ing sud - den - ly?___

w/Fill 1 (Gtr. 2) 1st time
w/Rhy. Fill 1 (Gtr. 2) 2nd time

_____ and all the choic - es that___ I___ make___ won't end up all___ for noth - ing.
_____ Will I ev - er get___ to___ see___ the end-ing to___ my sto - ry?___ }

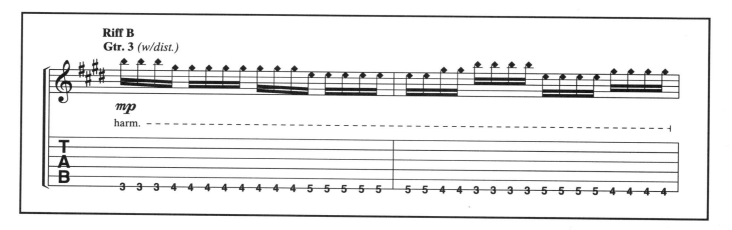

Riff B
Gtr. 3 (w/dist.)

mp
harm.

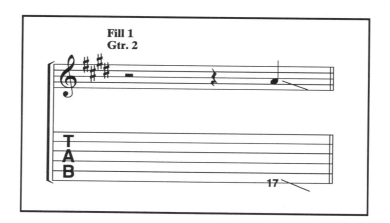

Fill 1
Gtr. 2

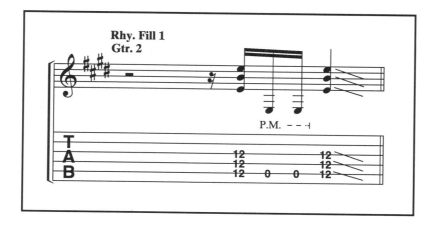

Rhy. Fill 1
Gtr. 2

P.M.

Chorus:
Gtr. 1 tacet
2nd time, Gtr. 3 tacet

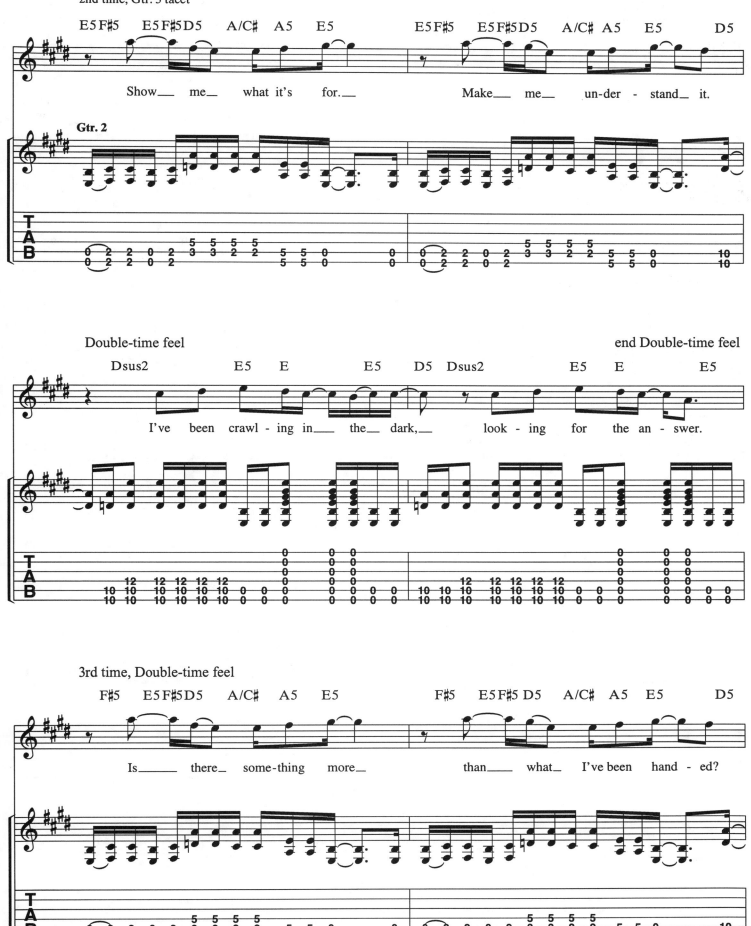

Show__ me__ what it's for.__ Make__ me__ un-der - stand__ it.

Gtr. 2

Double-time feel   **end Double-time feel**

I've been crawl - ing in__ the__ dark,__ look - ing for the an - swer.

3rd time, Double-time feel

Is_____ there__ some-thing more__ than_____ what__ I've been hand - ed?

64

Bridge:
w/misc. Bkgd. Vcls.

How much fur - ther do I have to___ go?___

And how much long - er till I fi - n'ly___ know?_

'Cause I'm look - ing and I just can't_ see___ what's___ in

66

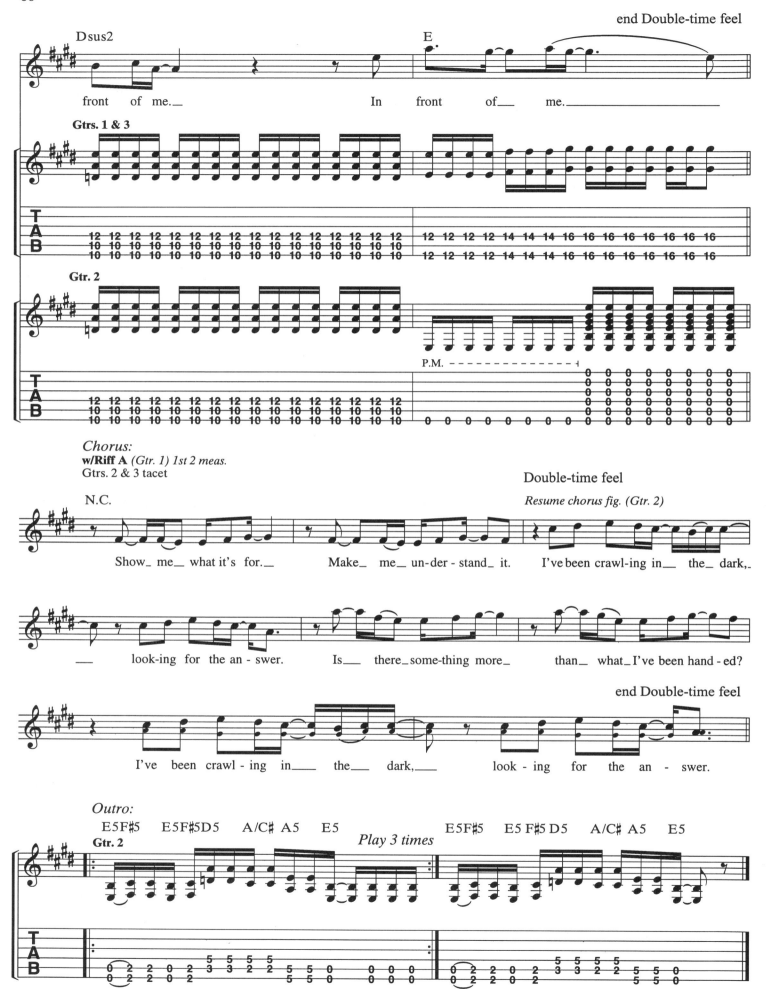

DECEMBER

Music and Lyrics by
ED ROLAND

FLY

All gtrs. tuned down 1/2 step:
⑥ = Eb ③ = Gb
⑤ = Ab ② = Bb
④ = Db ① = Eb

Words and Music by
MARK McGRATH, MURPHY KARGES, STAN FRAZIER,
RODNEY SHEPPARD, CRAIG BULLOCK and WILLIAM MARAGH

Moderately slow ska ♩ = 100
Intro:

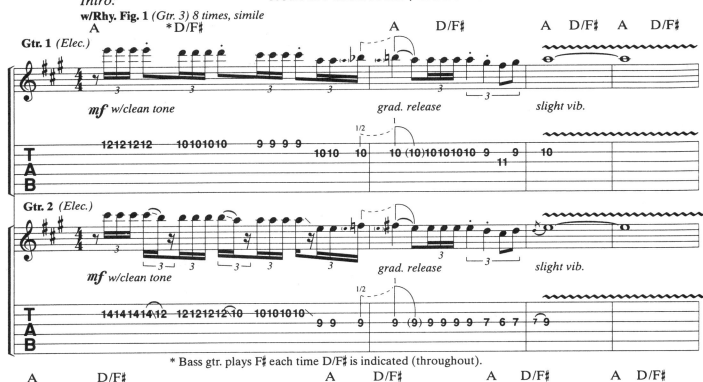

* Bass gtr. plays F# each time D/F# is indicated (throughout).

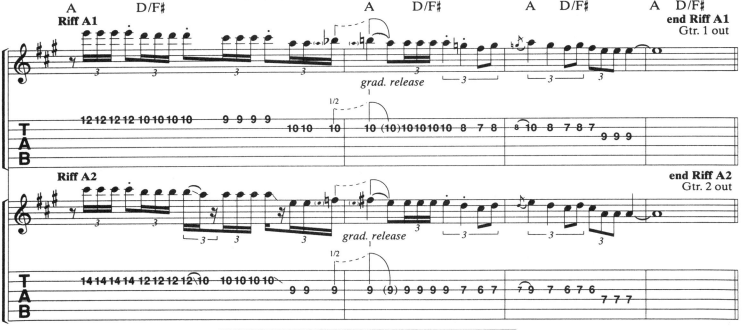

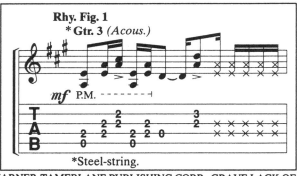

*Steel-string.

Verse 1:

74

Fly - 6 - 3

*Bass gtr. plays D each time Asus/D is indicated (throughout).

Interlude:
A5

* w/chorus and compression (next 4 bars).

Verse 3:
All around the world statues crumble for me.
Who knows how long I've loved you?
Everyone I know has been so good to me.
Twenty-five years old,
My mother, God rest her soul.
(To Chorus:)

GEL

Music and Lyrics by
ED ROLAND

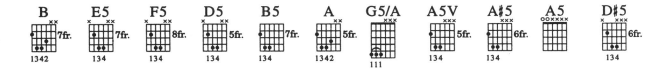

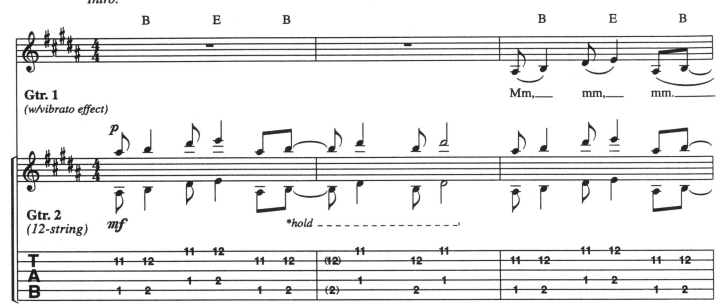

*Applies to both gtrs.

Gel - 8 - 1

*Vibrato effect off.

82

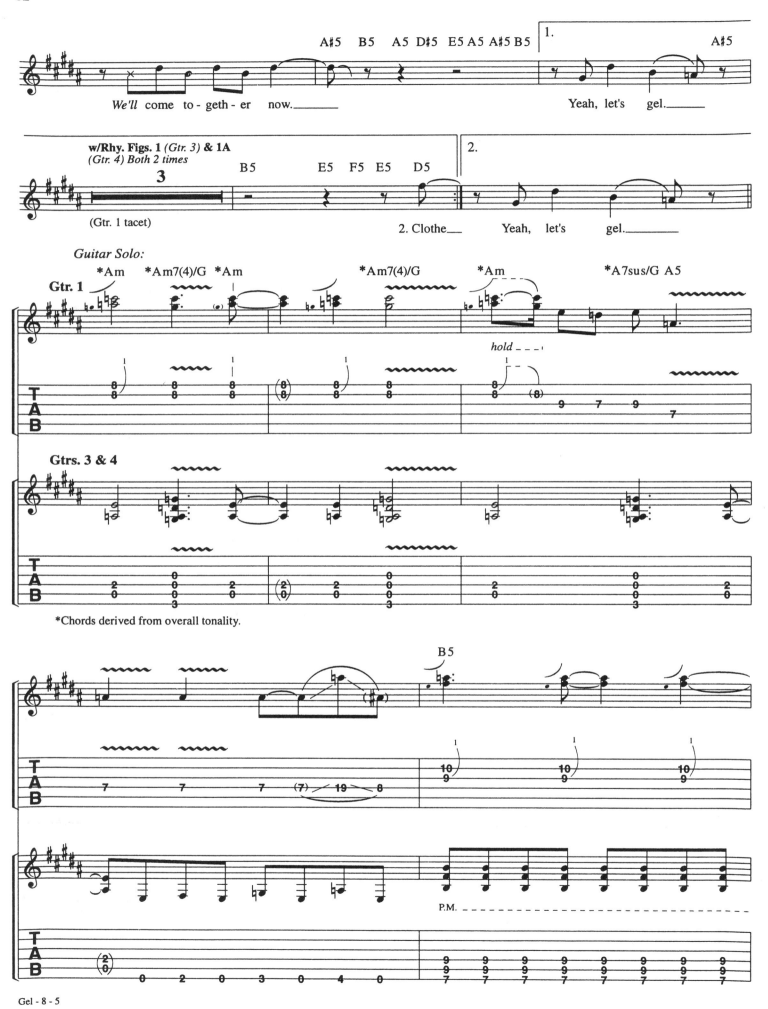

Gel - 8 - 5

84

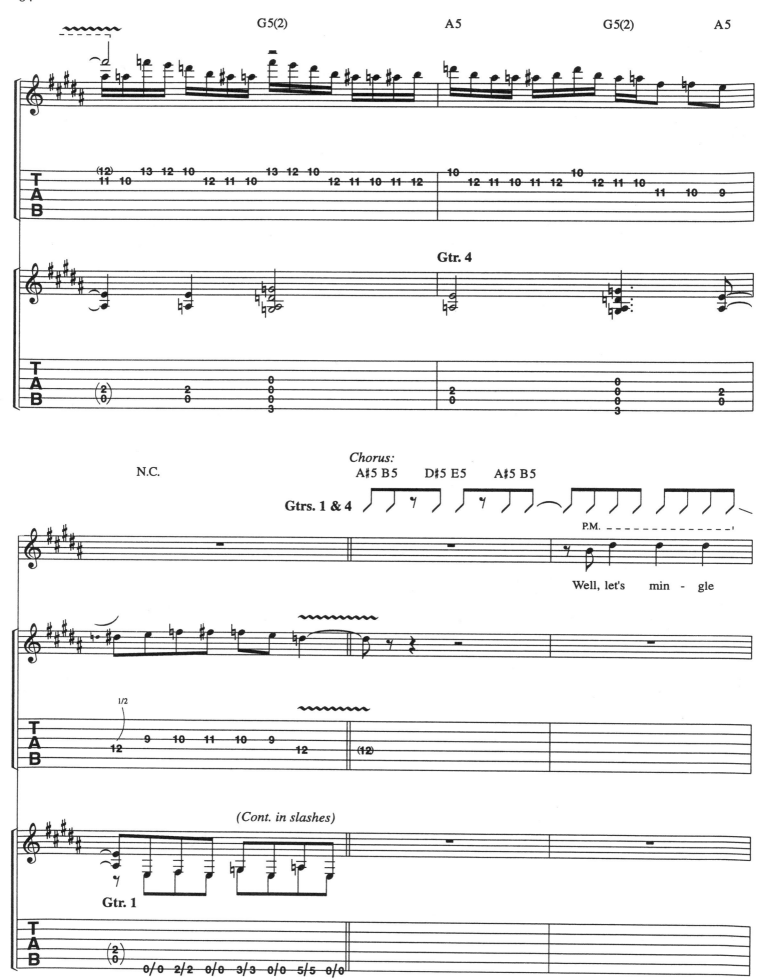

Gel - 8 - 7

Verse 2:
Clothe me in any fashion.
Glitter to so mundane.
Tell me how you'd love to change me.
Tell me I can stay the same.
Well, I just want to shake us up.
Well, I just want, I just-a want to,
To shake us up.
(To Chorus:)

86

THE GAME OF LOVE

Words and Music by
ALEX ANDER and RICK NOWELS

Composite arrangement.

The Game of Love - 11 - 1

© 2002 Keepin' It Real How 'Bout You Music, Future Furniture Music and EMI April Music Inc.
All Rights for Keepin' It Real How 'Bout You Music Administered
by Warner-Tamerlane Publishing Corp.
All Rights Reserved

88

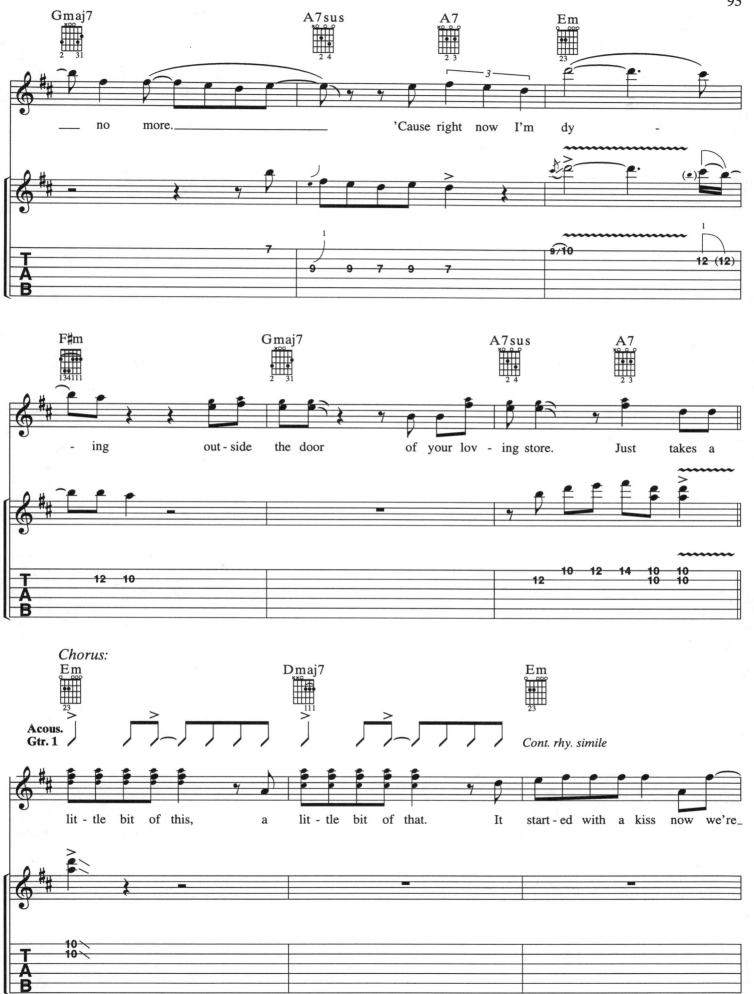

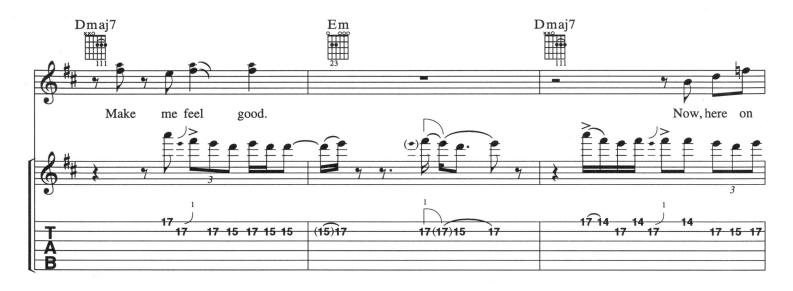

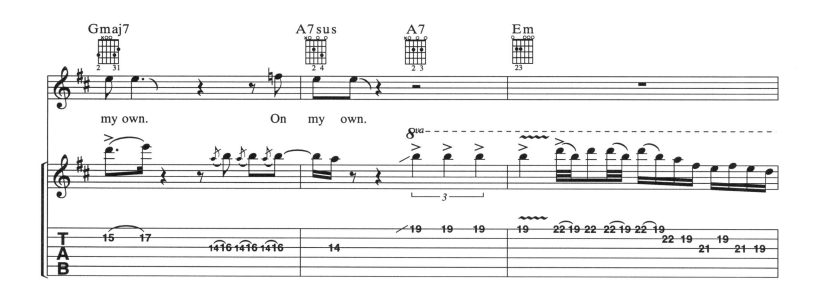

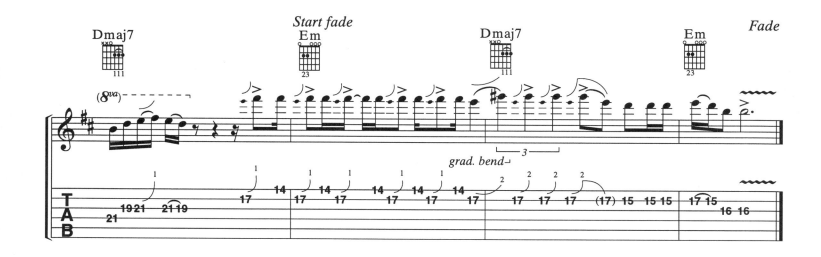

GOOD RIDDANCE (TIME OF YOUR LIFE)

Words and Music by
BILLIE JOE ARMSTRONG, FRANK WRIGHT
and MICHAEL PRITCHARD

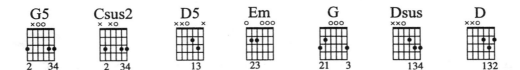

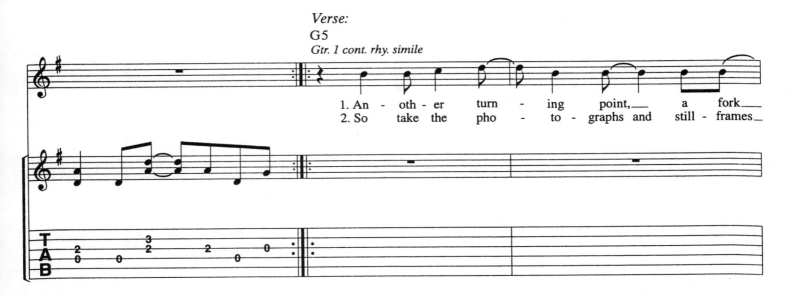

Good Riddance (Time of Your Life) - 3 - 1

98

Good Riddance (Time of Your Life) - 3 - 2

GOING UNDER

Elec. Gtr. 1 tuned:
⑥ = B ③ = D
⑤ = E ② = G
④ = A ① = B

Written by Ben Moody,
Amy Lee and David Hodges

102

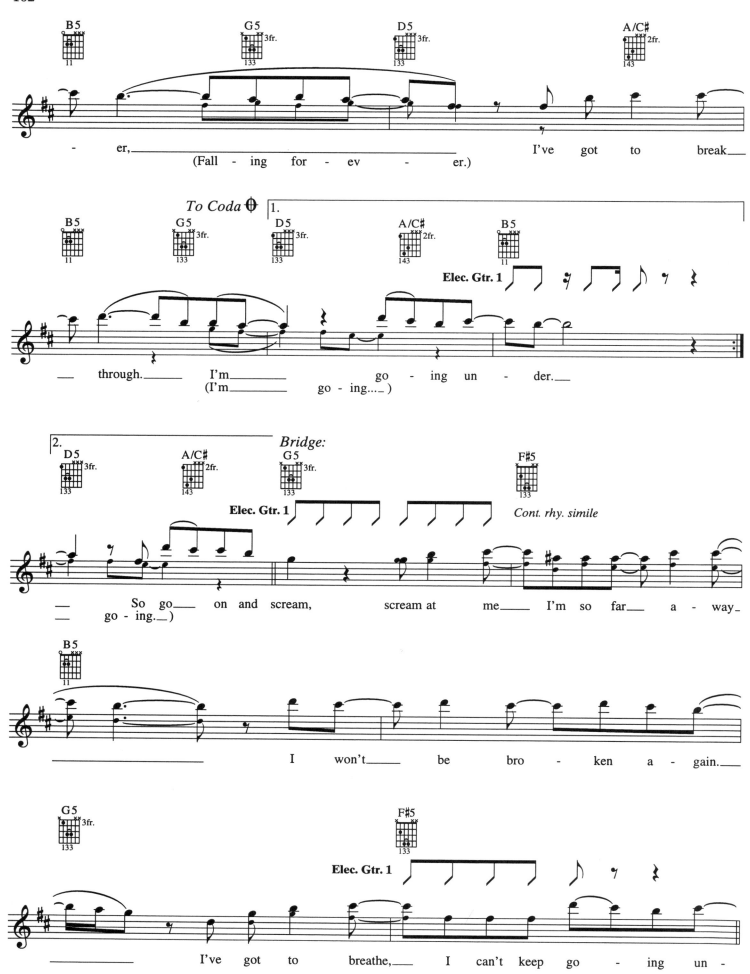

Going Under - 4 - 3

103

Going Under - 4 - 4

HOW YOU REMIND ME

Lyrics by CHAD KROEGER
Music by NICKELBACK

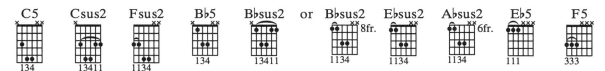

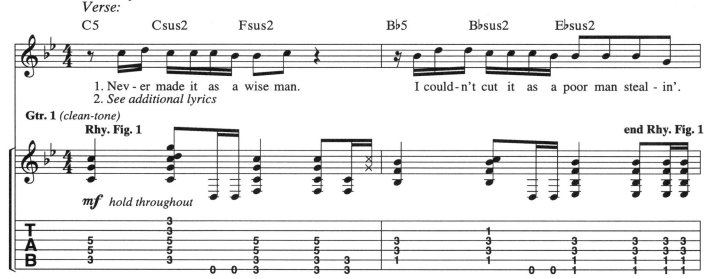

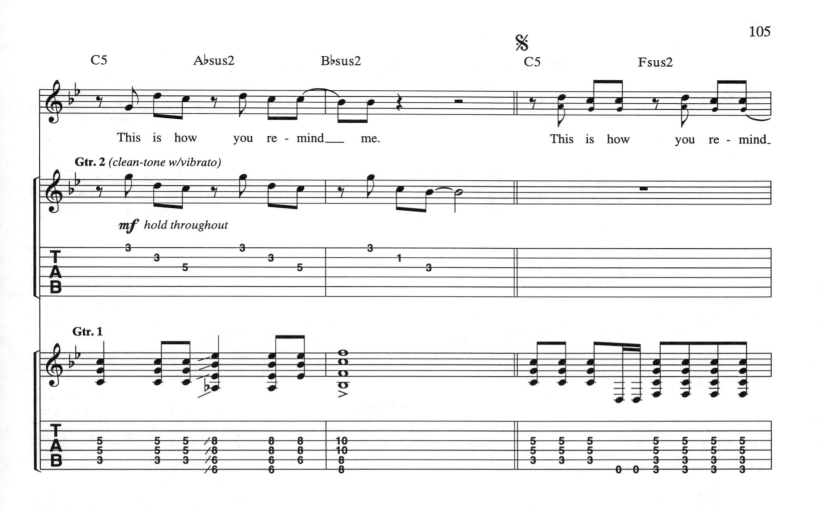

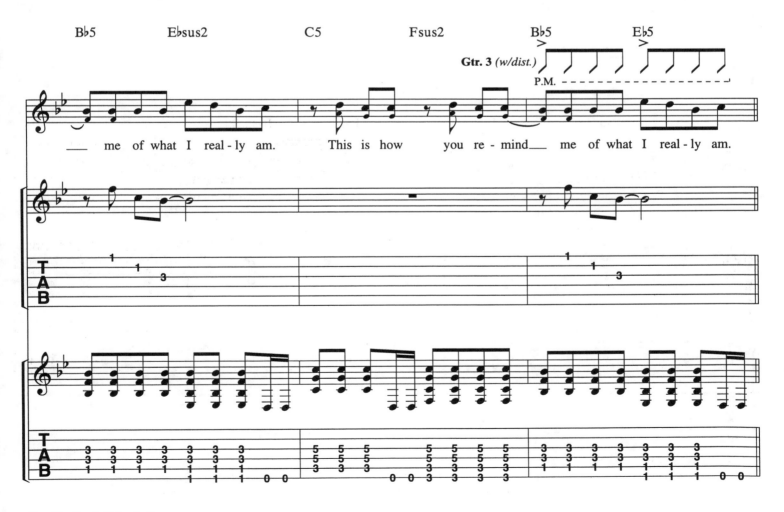

Chorus:

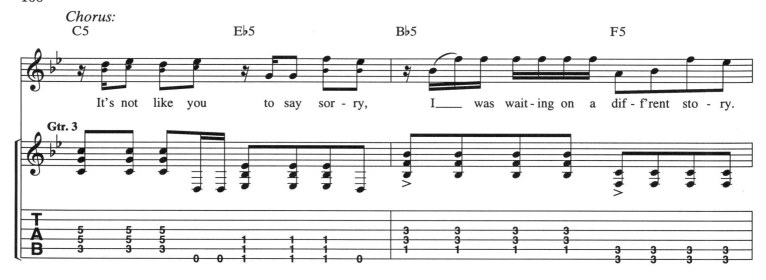

It's not like you to say sor - ry, I___ was wait - ing on a dif - f'rent sto - ry.

Play slash chord on D.S. only.

This time I'm mis - tak - en for hand - ing you a heart worth break - ing.

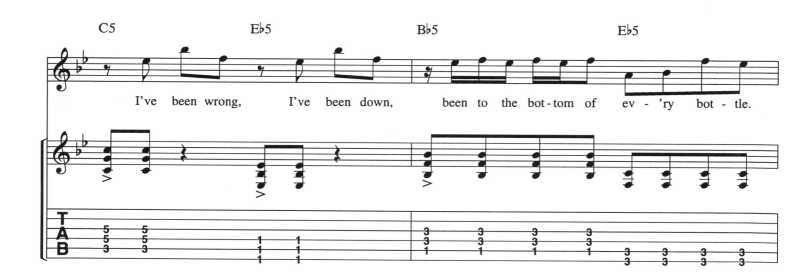

I've been wrong, I've been down, been to the bot - tom of ev - 'ry bot - tle.

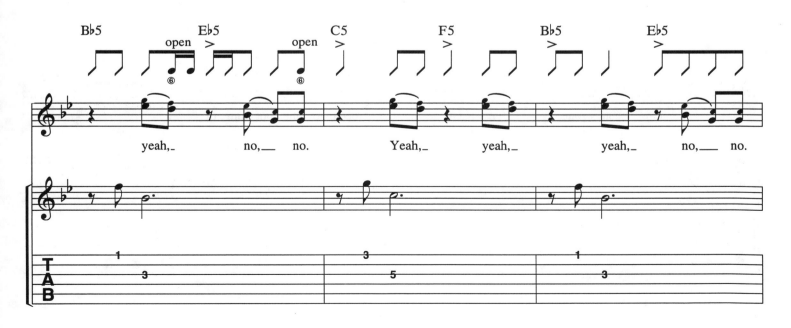

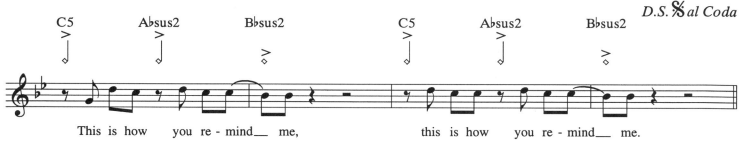

Verse 2:
It's not like you didn't know that.
I said I love you and I swear I still do.
And it must have been so bad.
'Cause livin' with me must have damn near killed you.

This is how you remind me of what I really am.
This is how you remind me of what I really am.
(To Chorus:)

I'D DO ANYTHING

All gtrs. tuned down ½ step:

⑥ = E♭ ③ = G♭
⑤ = A♭ ② = B♭
④ = D♭ ① = E♭

Words and Music by CHARLES-ANDRE COMEAU,
JEAN-FRANCOIS STINCO,
PIERRE BOUVIER, SEBASTIEN LEFEBVRE
and ARNOLD LANNI

Fast ♩ = 164
Intro:

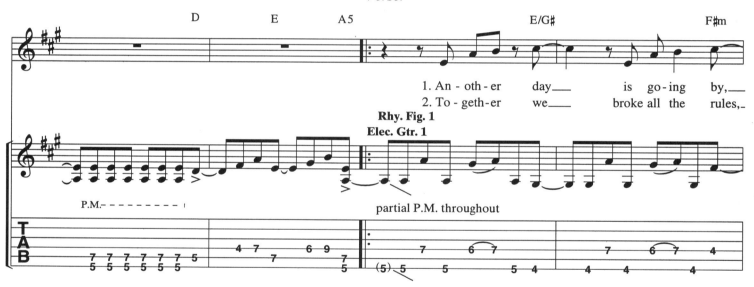

*Recording sounds a half step lower than written.

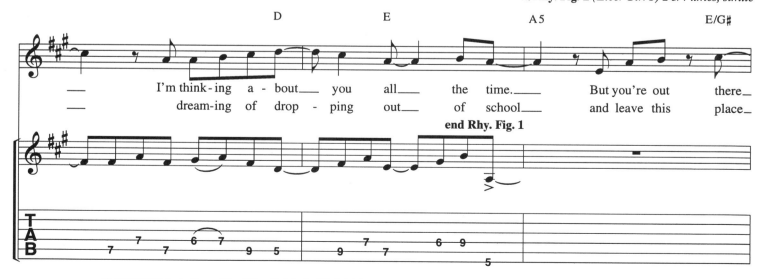

112

I'd Do Anything - 8 - 3

114

HEADSTRONG

Music by
CHRIS BROWN, PETER CHARELL
and SIMON ORMANDY
Lyrics by
CHRIS BROWN

Double-time feel
w/Riff A *(6-string Gtr. 1)*
7-string Gtr. tacet

1. Cir - cl - ing, you're cir - cl - ing, you're

Verse:
w/Riff A *(6-string Gtr. 1) 4 times*

cir - cl - ing your head, con - tem - plat - ing ev - 'ry - thing you ev - er said. Now I see the
clu - sions man - i - fest your first im - pres - sion's got to be your ver - y best. I see you're full of

end Double-time feel

truth I got a doubt. A dif - f'rent mo - tive in your eyes and now I'm out, see you lat - er.
shit and that's al - right. That's how you play, I guess, you get through ev - 'ry night. Well, now that's o - ver.

I see your fan - ta - sy, you wan - na make it a re - al - i - ty paved in gold.

See in - side, in - side of our heads, yeah. Well, now that's o - ver, I see your

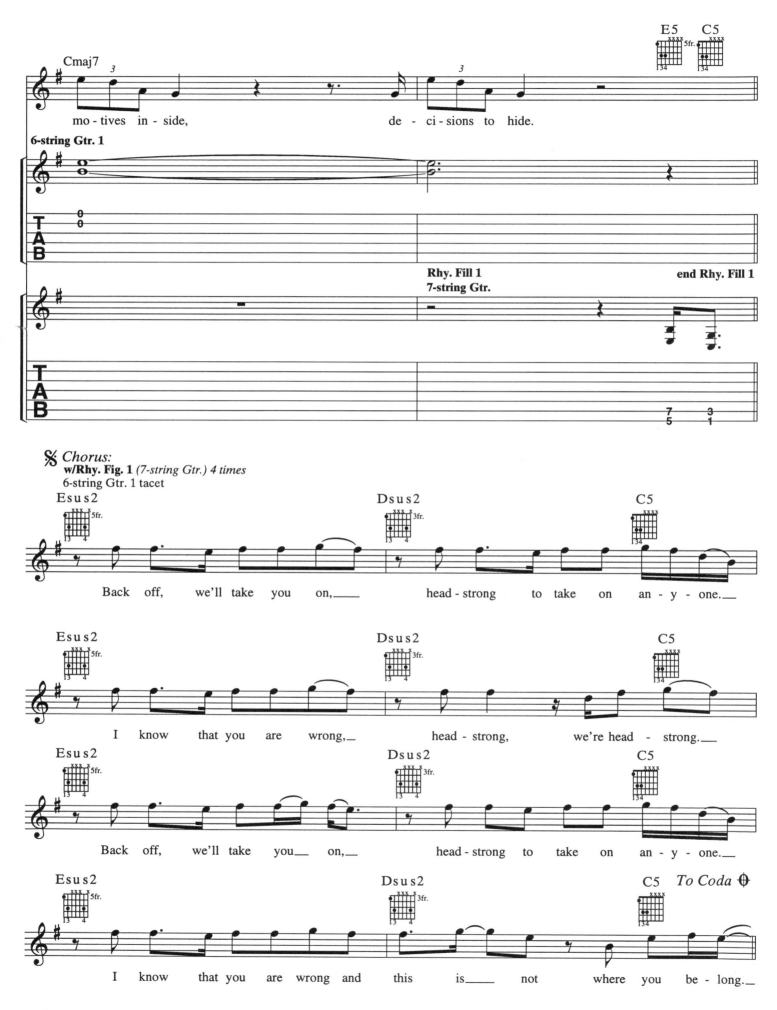

122

Headstrong - 7 - 5

w/Riff B *(6-string Gtr. 2) 2 times*

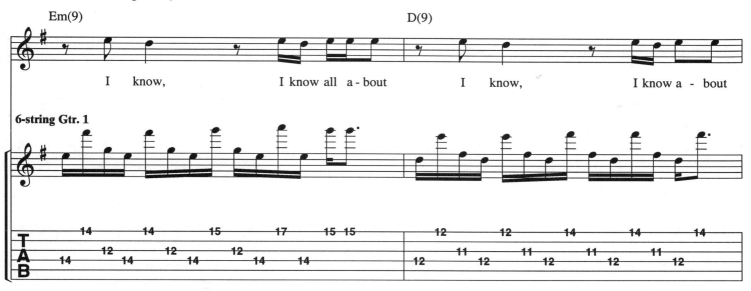

I know,   I know all a-bout   I know,   I know a-bout

end Double-time feel

I know,   I know all a-bout.   I know,   I know all a-bout your

D.S. 𝄋 al Coda

6-string Gtrs. 1 & 2 tacet   **w/Rhy. Fill 1** *(7-string Gtr.)*

mo-tives in-side,   and your de-ci-sion to hide.

KARMA POLICE

Words and Music by
THOMAS YORKE, JONATHAN GREENWOOD, PHILIP SELWAY,
COLIN GREENWOOD and EDWARD O'BRIEN

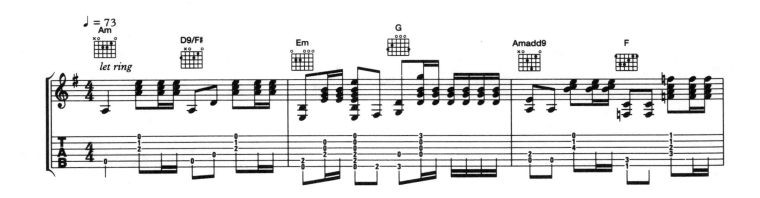

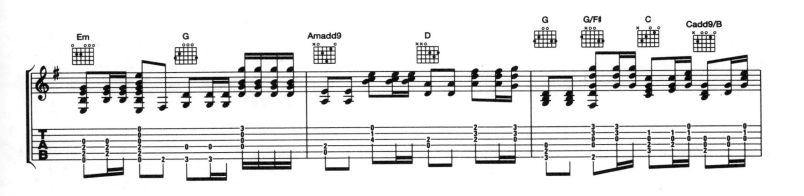

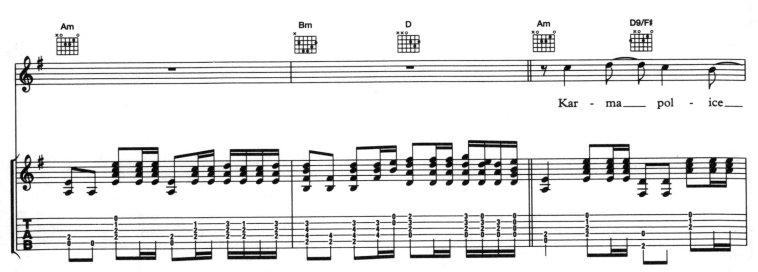

Kar - ma___ pol - ice___

Karma Police - 5 - 1

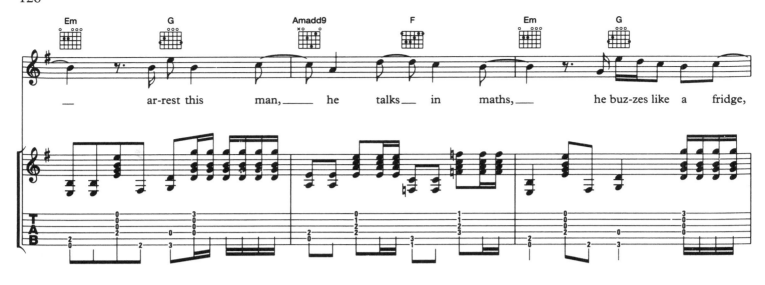

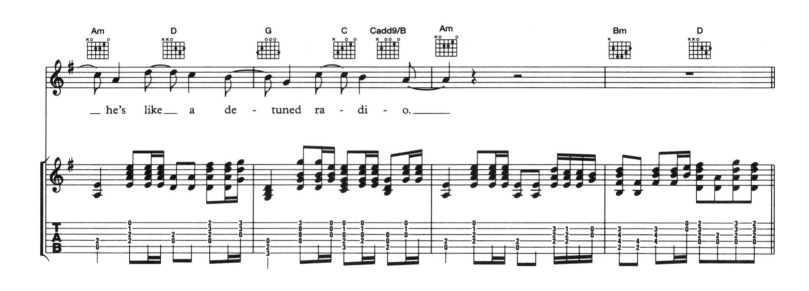

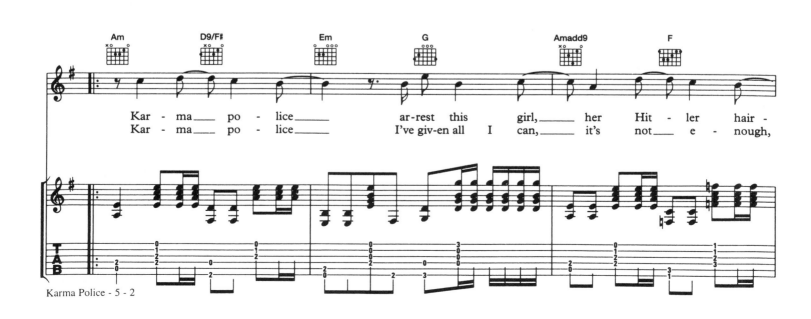

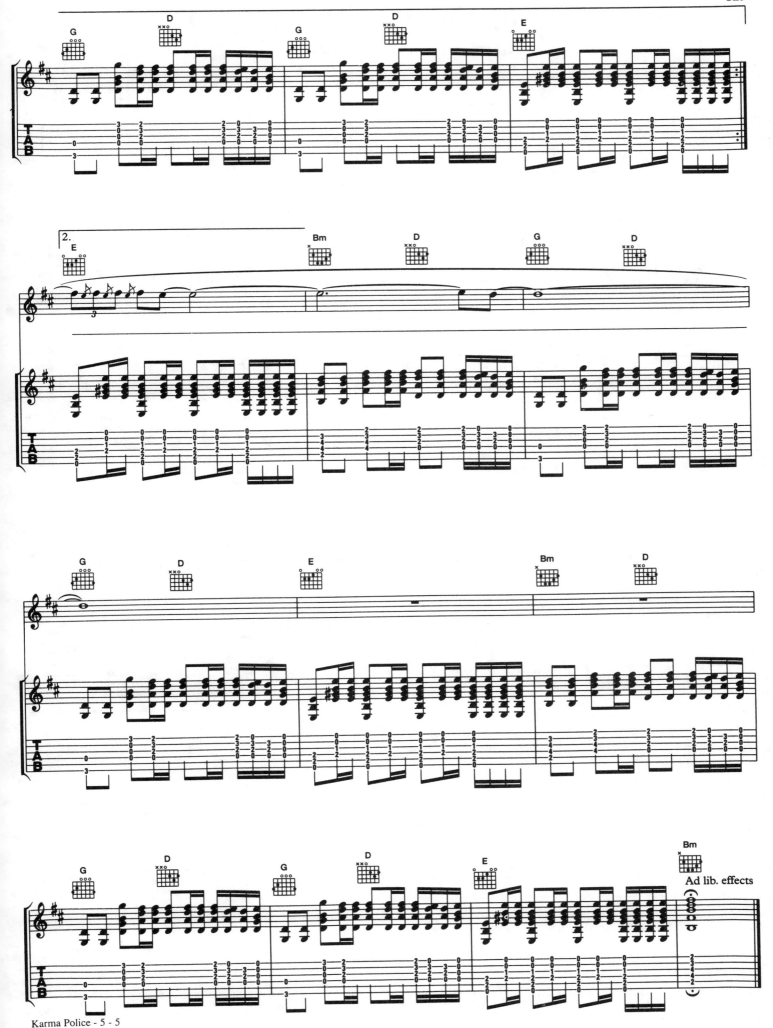

Karma Police - 5 - 5

IF IT MAKES YOU HAPPY

Words and Music by
SHERYL CROW
and JEFF TROTT

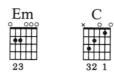

*Gtr. 1 (Elec.), Gtr. 2 (Acoustic), open G tuning: ⑥= D, ⑤= G, ④= D, ③= G, ②= B, ①= D.

* Open G tuning: ⑥= D, ⑤= G, ④= D, ③= G, ②= B, ①= D.

If It Makes You Happy - 6 - 1

If It Makes You Happy - 6 - 2

Pre-Chorus:

I made this up.
2.3. *See additional lyrics*
I prom-ised you I'd nev-er give up.___ If it makes you hap-

Gtrs. 1 & 2

Gtr. 3

Gtr. 3 out

Chorus:

- py,___ it can't be that bad._____ If it makes you hap-

Gtrs. 1 & 2
Rhy. Fig. 3

1. w/Rhy. Fig. 1 *(Gtrs. 1 & 2) 2 times*

- py,___ then why the hell are you___ so___ sad?

end Rhy. Fig. 3

134

Verse 3:
You get down, real low down.
You listen to Coltrane, derail your own train.
Well, who hasn't been there before?

Verse 4:
I come 'round, around the hard way.
Bring you comics in bed, scrape the mold off the bread,
And serve you French toast again.

Pre-Chorus 3:
Well, o.k., we get along.
So what if right now everything's wrong?
(To Chorus:)

Pre-Chorus 2:
Well, o.k., I still get stoned.
I'm not the kind of girl you'd take home.
(To Chorus:)

Verse 5:
We've been far, far away from here.
Put on a poncho, played for mosquitoes,
And everywhere in between.

If It Makes You Happy - 6 - 6

NEW FOUND POWER

All gtrs. in Drop D, down 2 steps:

⑥ = B♭ ③ = E♭
⑤ = F ② = G
④ = B♭ ① = C

Words and Music by
DARRELL ABBOTT, VINCENT ABBOTT
and PATRICK LACHMAN

Moderately ♩. = 82

*Recording sounds a major third lower than written.

138

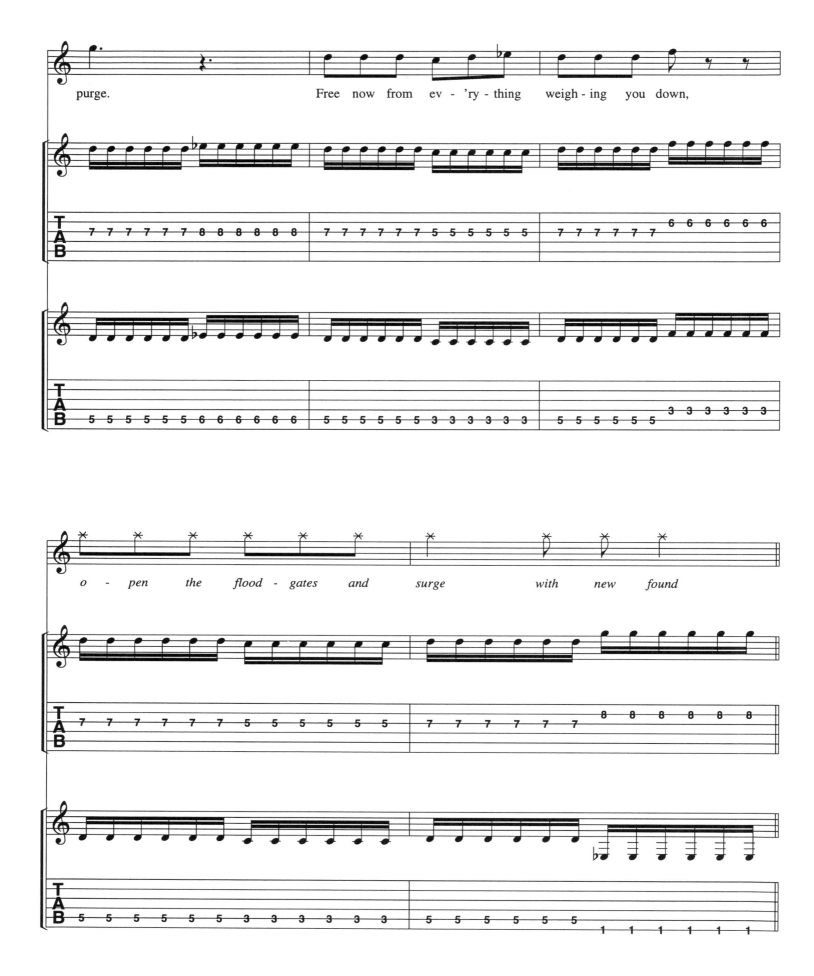

purge.　　　Free now from ev - 'ry - thing　weigh - ing　you down,

o - pen　the　flood - gates　and　surge　with　new　found

140

142

ONE THING

All gtrs. in Drop D, down 1/2 step:

⑥ = D♭   ③ = G♭
⑤ = A♭   ② = B♭
④ = D♭   ① = E♭

Words and Music by
SCOTT ANDERSON and JAMES BLACK

Moderately slow ♩ = 76

Intro:

Play 4 times

A5   A6   D(9)/A   A5

Rhy. Fig. 1

Acous. Gtr. 1

mf

fingerstyle
hold throughout

Recording sounds a half step lower than written.

Verses 1 & 2:
w/Rhy. Fig. 1 *(Acous. Gtr. 1) 4 times*

A5   A6   D(9)/A   A5

1. Rest - less to - night_ 'cause I wast - ed the_ light._ Be-
   prom - ise I_ might_ not walk on_ by._

A6   D(9)/A   A5

tween both these times_ I drew a real - ly thin line. It's
May - be next time,_ but not this time.

A6   D(9)/A   A5

noth - ing I planned_ and not that I_ can._ But
E - ven though I know, I don't wan - na know.

One Thing - 4 - 1

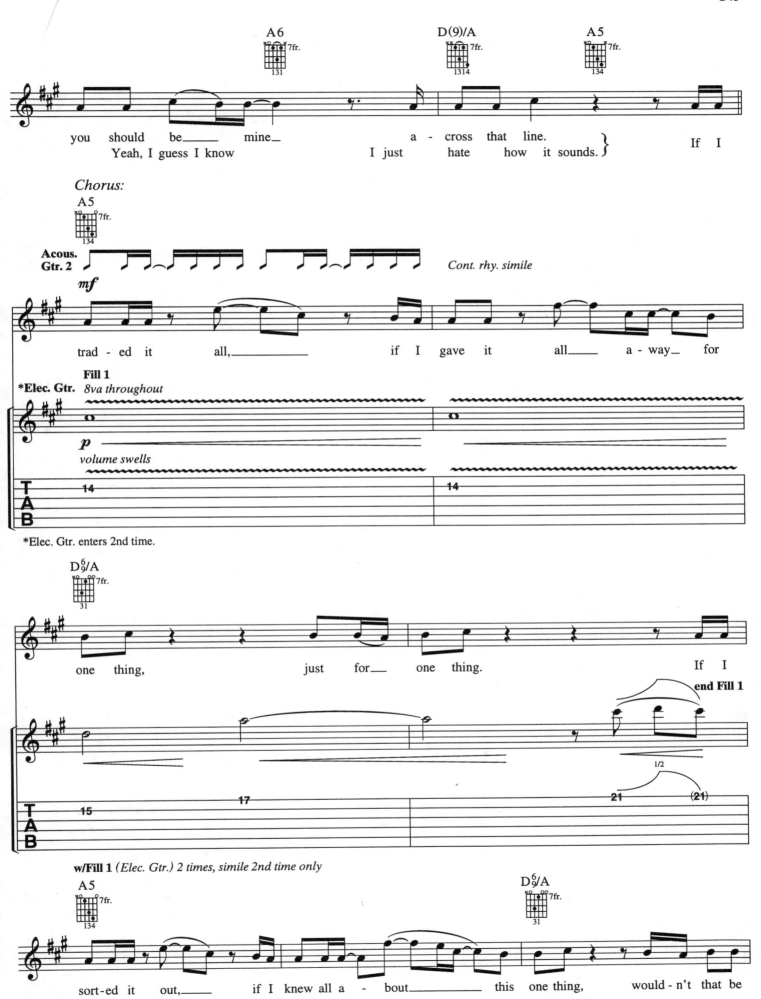

MY FAVORITE MISTAKE

Words and Music by
SHERYL CROW and JEFF TROTT

Moderate rock ♩ = 104

Fill 1
Gtr. 3
w/tremolo effect

You're my fa - v'rite mis - take._____ Well,

Bridge:

154

My Favorite Mistake - 7 - 7

ONE HEADLIGHT

Words and Music by
JAKOB DYLAN

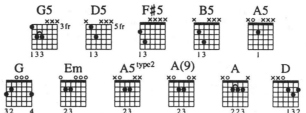

Gtr. 1 tuned: Gtr. 3 (Dobro) tuned:

⑥- D   ③- G   ⑥- D   ③- G
⑤- A   ②- B   ⑤- G   ②- B
④- D   ①- E   ④- D   ①- D

Moderately ♩ = 106

Intro:

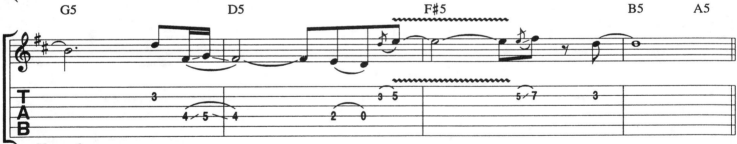

Verse 1:

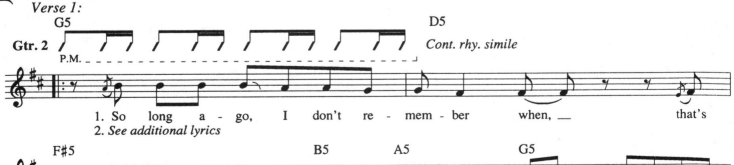

1. So long a - go, I don't re - mem - ber when, ___ that's
2. *See additional lyrics*

when they say I lost _ my on - ly friend. _ Well, they said she died eas - y of a

One Headlight – 7 – 1

*Gtrs. 1 & 3 ad lib. simile on Verse 4.

One Headlight – 7 – 5

Outro:

*Ad lib. simile on repeats.

Verse 2:
I seen the sun comin' up at the funeral at dawn,
Of the long broken arm of human law.
Now, it always seemed such a waste,
She always had a pretty face;
I wondered why she hung around this place.
(To Chorus:)

Verse 5:
This place is old, and it feels just like a beat-up truck.
I turn the engine, but the engine doesn't turn.
It smells of cheap wine and cigarettes,
This place is always such a mess;
Sometimes I think I'd like to watch it burn.

Verse 6:
Now I sit alone, and I feel just like somebody else.
Man, I ain't changed, but I know I ain't the same.
But somewhere here, in between these city walls of dying dreams,
I think her death, it must be killing me.
(To Chorus:)

One Headlight – 7 – 7

PRAYER

Words and Music by
**DAVID DRAIMAN, DAN DONEGAN,
FUZZ and MIKE WENGREN**

All gtrs. tune down 1/2 step w/Drop D tuning:

⑥ = D♭ ③ = G♭
⑤ = A♭ ② = B♭
④ = D♭ ① = E♭

♩ = 98   *Intro:*

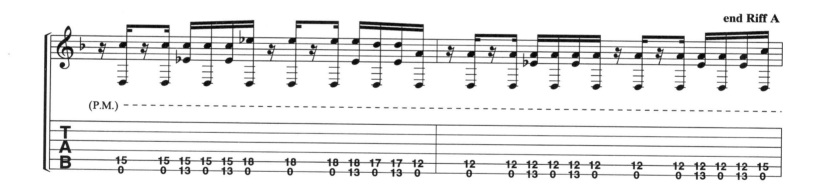

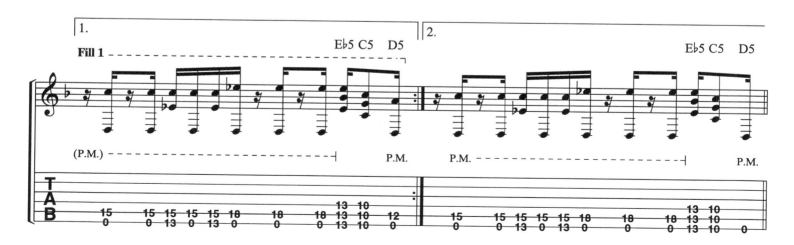

Pre-chorus:

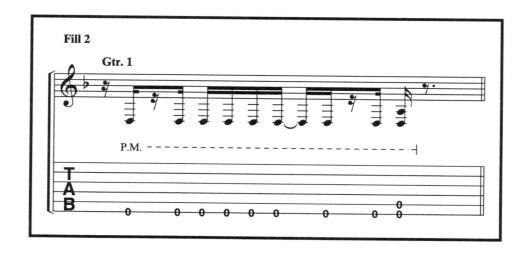

PRICE TO PLAY

Music by MICHAEL MUSHOK,
AARON LEWIS, JOHN APRIL
and JONATHAN WYSOCKI
Lyrics by AARON LEWIS

All gtrs. tuned to:
⑥ = F#   ③ = C#
⑤ = C#   ② = F#
④ = G#   ① = A#

Moderately ♩ = 112

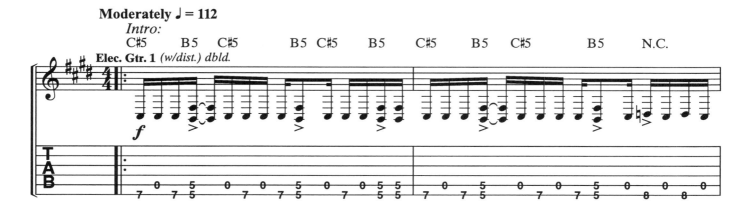

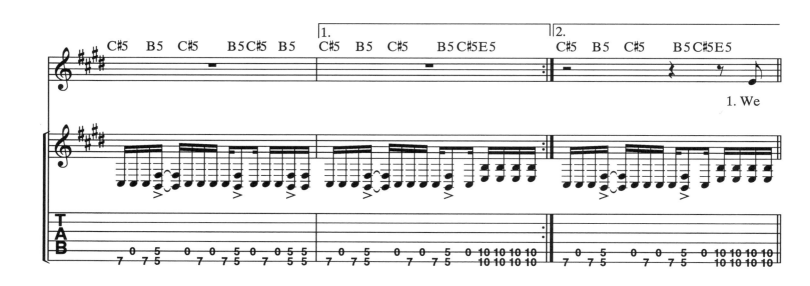

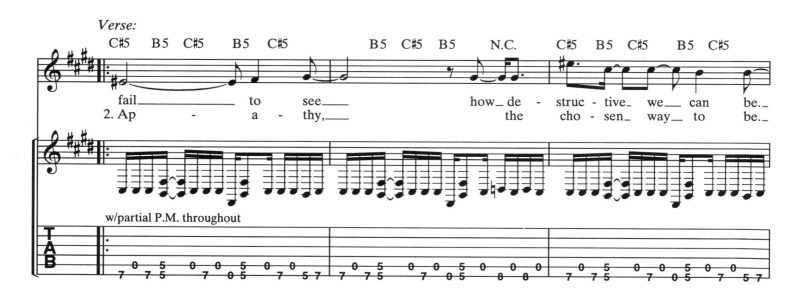

the game. What you pay to play the game.

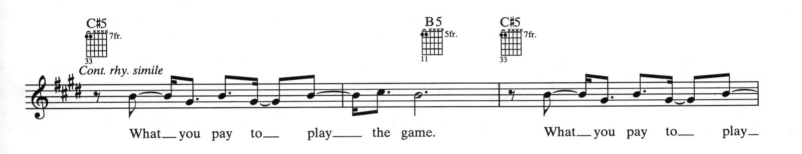

What you pay to play the game. What you pay to play

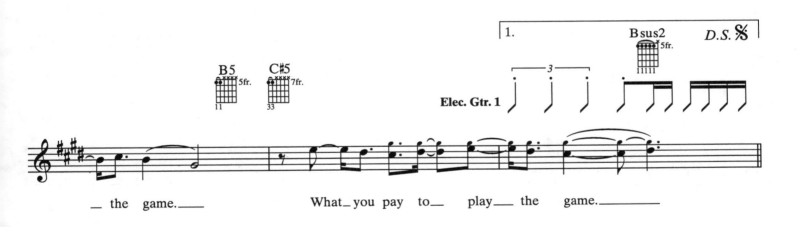

the game. What you pay to play the game.

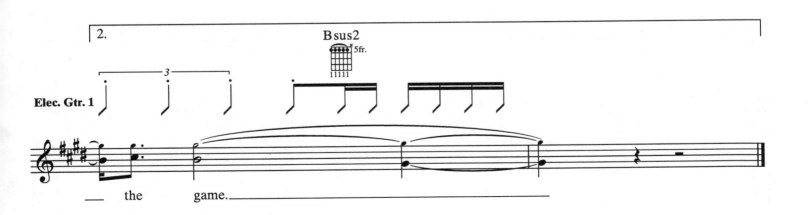

the game.

ONE WEEK

Words and Music by
ED ROBERTSON

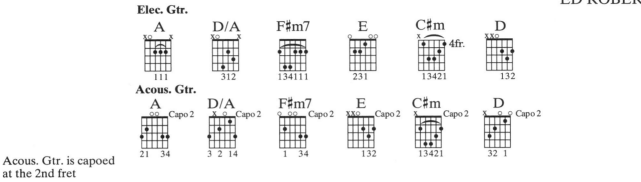

Acous. Gtr. is capoed
at the 2nd fret

Moderate rock ♩ = 112

Chorus 1:
w/Rhy. Fill 1 *(Gtr. 4)* 8 times

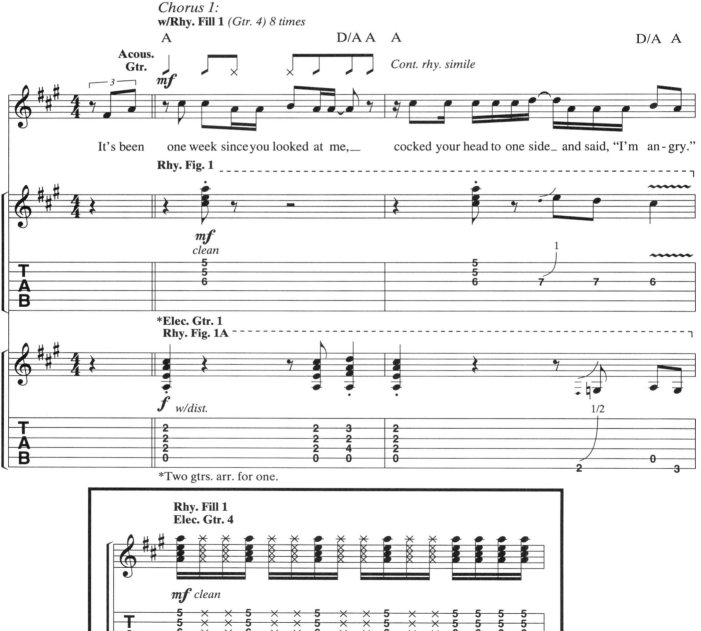

It's been   one week since you looked at me,___ cocked your head to one side_ and said, "I'm an-gry."

*Two gtrs. arr. for one.

S Verse:
w/Rhy. Fill 1 *(Elec. Gtr. 3) 12 times*

1. Hold it now and watch the hood-wink as I make you stop, think. You'll think you're look-ing at Aq-ua-man.
2. Chick-i-ty Chi-na, the Chi-nese chick-en, you have a drum-stick and your brain stops tick-in'.

Ending of Interlude

*Elec. Gtr. 1 Verse 2 only.

One Week - 9 - 3

181

One Week - 9 - 8

182

Birch-mount Sta - d'um, home_ of the Rob - bie.

SAVE TONIGHT

Words and Music by
EAGLE-EYE CHERRY

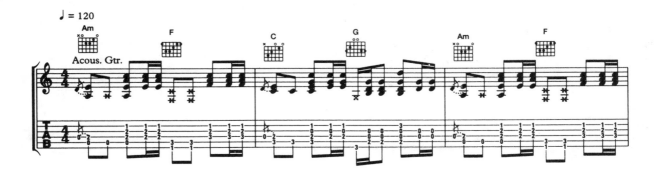

Doo dun doo doo   doo dun doo doo

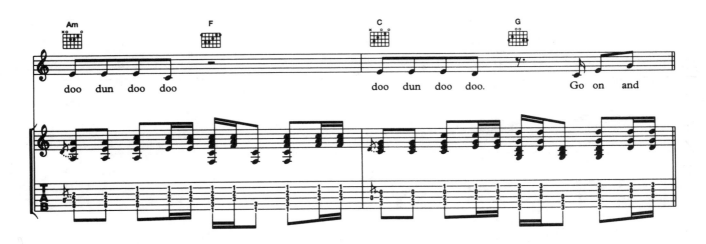

doo dun doo doo   doo dun doo doo.   Go on and

Save Tonight - 7 - 1

184

186

Save Tonight - 7 - 4

Save Tonight - 7 - 5

188

repeat ad lib. to fade

Save Tonight - 7 - 7

THE REASON

Music by DAN ESTRIN
Lyrics by DOUG ROBB

Moderately ♩ = 78
Intro:

*Implied harmony.

Verses 1 & 2:

†Verse 2 only.

A

And so I have to say before I go
And be the one who catch-es all your

B

tears.
I
that I just want you to know
That's why I need you to hear.

Elec. Gtr. 1

end Rhy. Fig. 1

Elec. Gtr. 2 *(w/dist.)*

f

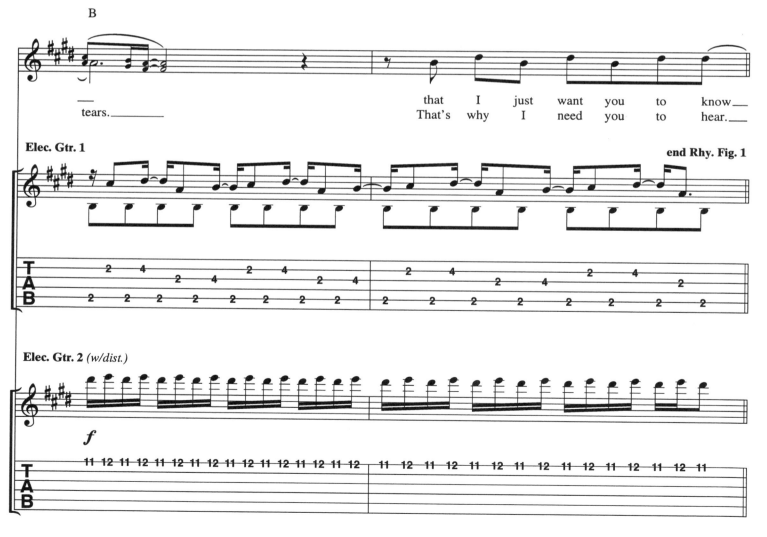

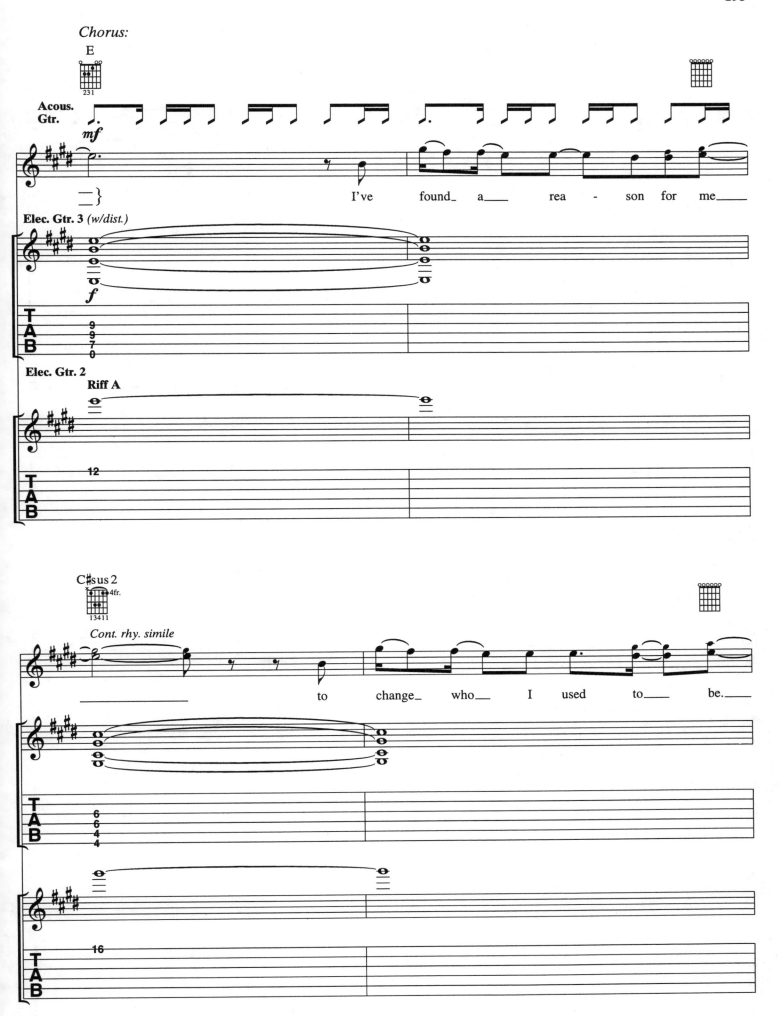

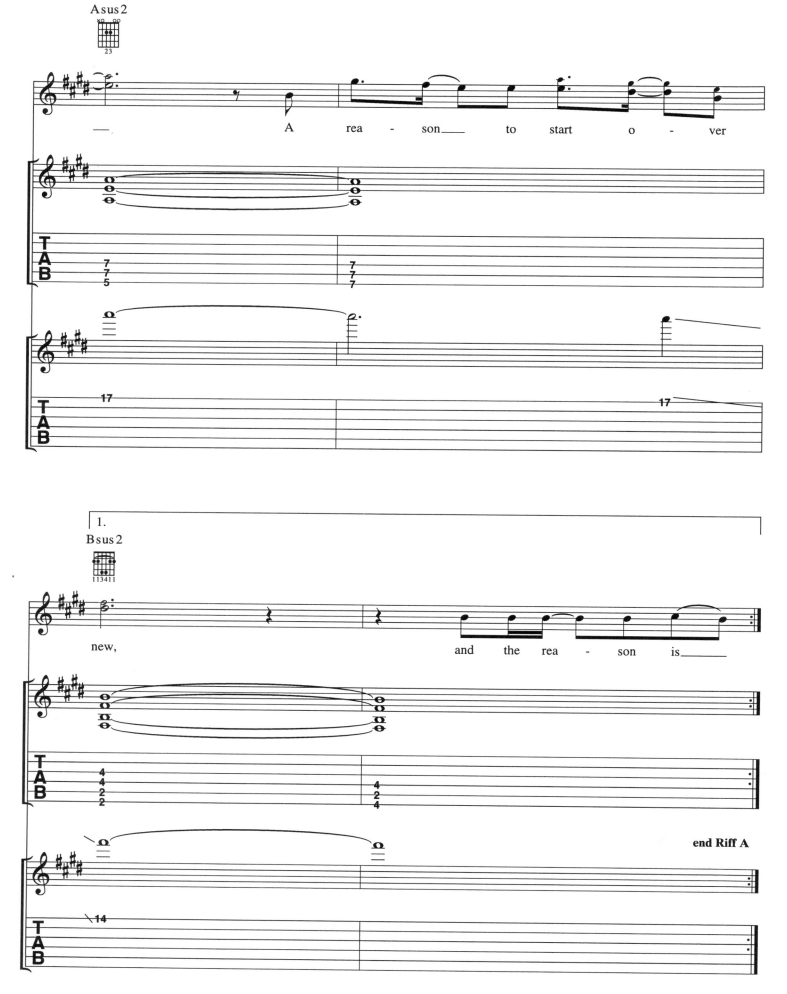

196

The Reason - 12 - 10

THE RED

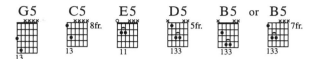

Words by PETE LOEFFLER
Music by CHEVELLE

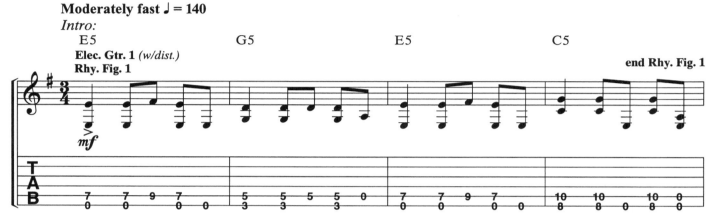

*Music sounds a min. 3rd lower than written.

Verse 1:

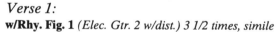

The Red - 6 - 2

204

SEND THE PAIN BELOW

*All gtrs. in Drop D, down 1 1/2 steps:

⑥ = B   ③ = E
⑤ = F#   ② = G#
④ = B   ① = C#

Words by PETE LOEFFLER
Music by CHEVELLE

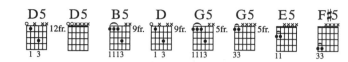

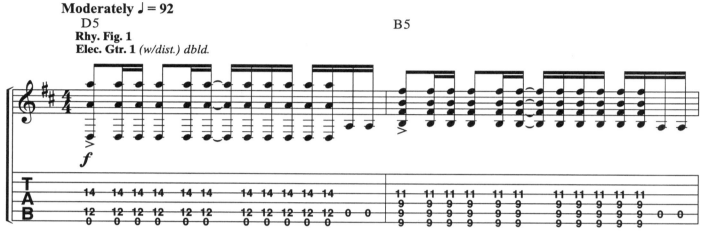

*Music sounds a min. 3rd lower than written.

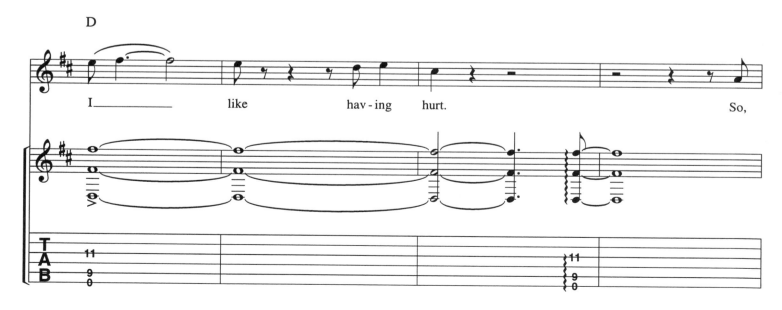

I_____ like hav-ing hurt. So,

Send the Pain Below - 4 - 1

*F♯ played by bass gtr. only.

Send the Pain Below - 4 - 2

210

SEX AND CANDY

Words and Music by
JOHN WOZNIAK

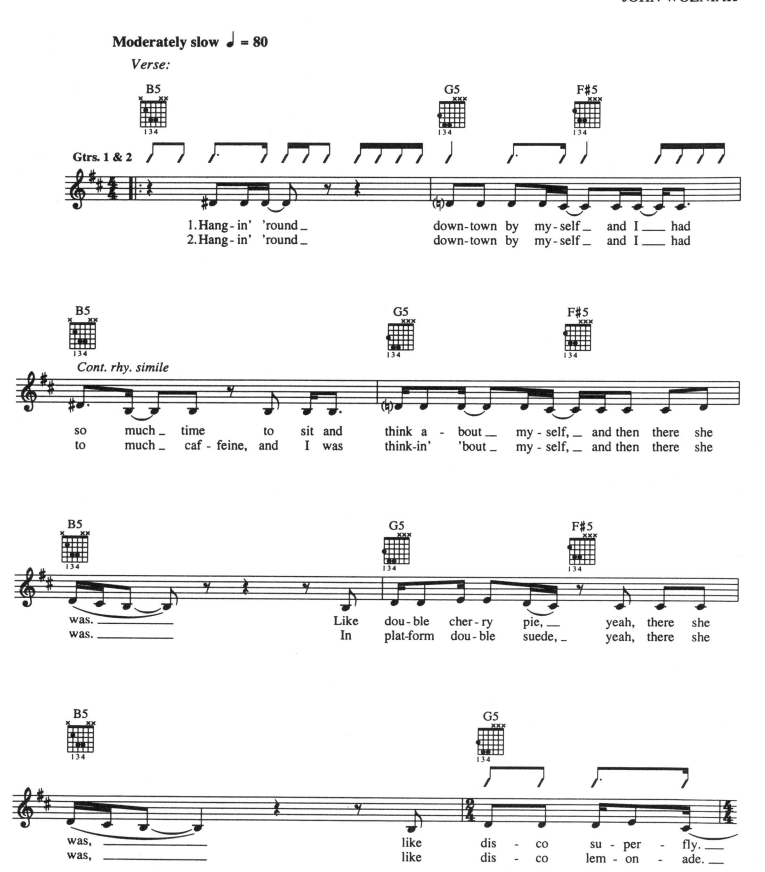

Sex and Candy – 3 – 1

Sex and Candy – 3 – 2

214

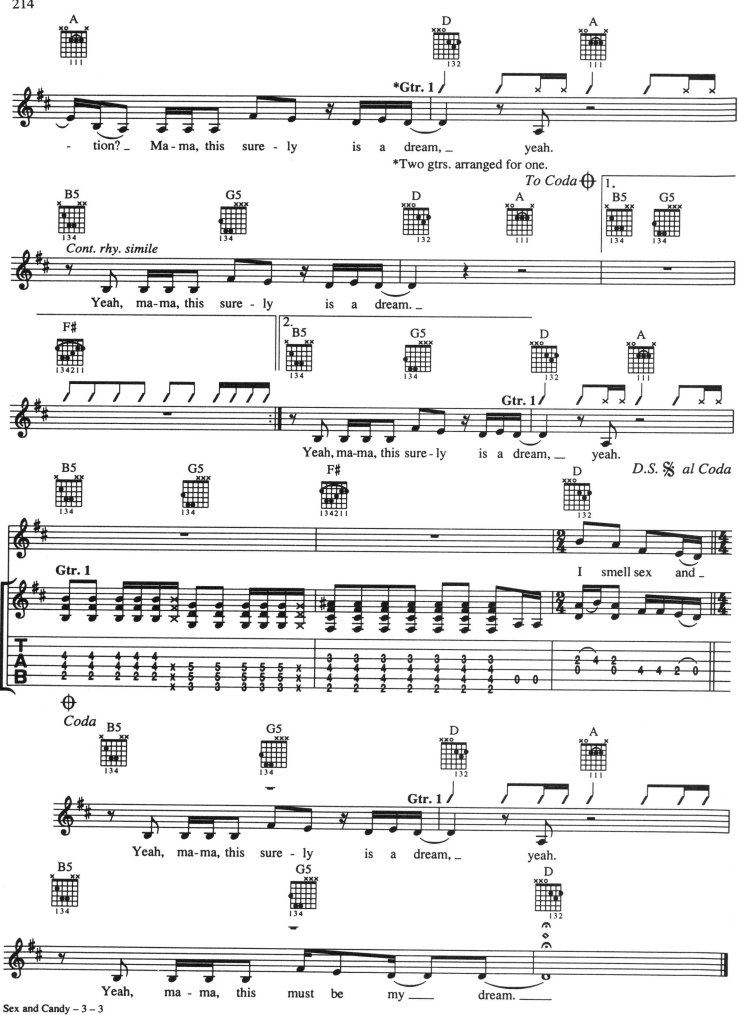

Sex and Candy – 3 – 3

6th AVENUE HEARTACHE

Words and Music by
JAKOB DYLAN

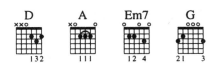

Gtr. 2 in G tuning:
⑥ - D ③ - G
⑤ - G ② - B
④ - D ① - D

Gtrs. 1 & 3 Capo III

Moderately ♩ = 96

Intro:

6th Avenue Heartache – 9 – 1

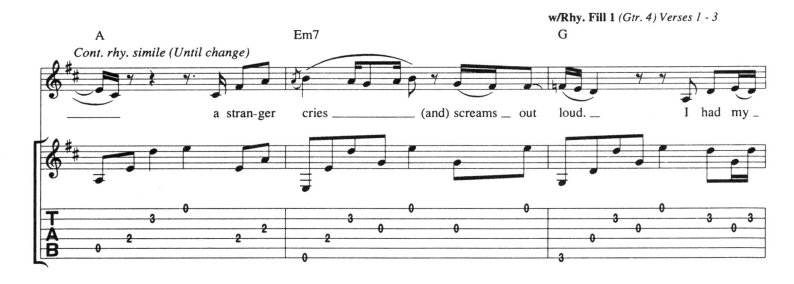

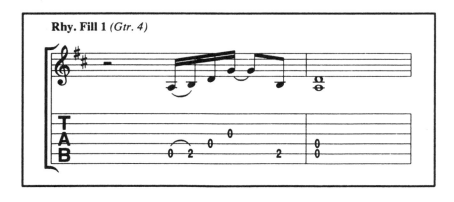

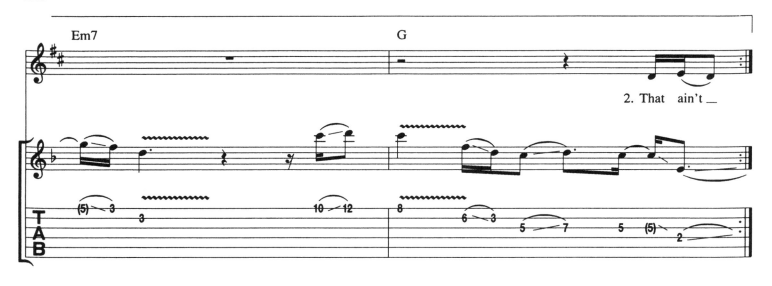

Em7　　　　　　　　　　　　　　　G

2. That ain't __

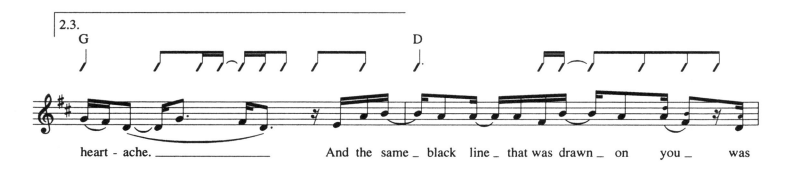

2.3.
G　　　　　　　　　　　　　　　D

heart - ache. _____　And the same _ black line _ that was drawn _ on　you _　was

A　　　　　　　　　　　　　Em7　　　　　　　To Coda ⊕

drawn on　me, _____ and now it's draw-in' me in. _____

Well, Sixth Av - e - nue

w/Rhy. Fig. 1 *(Gtr. 2) simile*

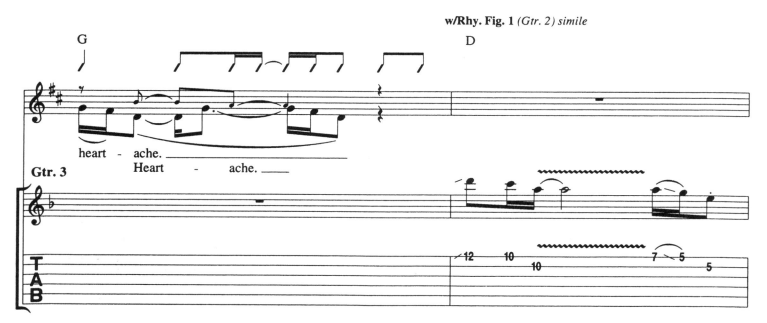

G　　　　　　　　　　　　　　　D

heart - ache. _____
Heart - ache. _____

Gtr. 3

220

Verse 4:

Chorus:
w/Rhy. Fig. 2 *(Gtrs. 3 & 4) simile until end*

Gtr. 3

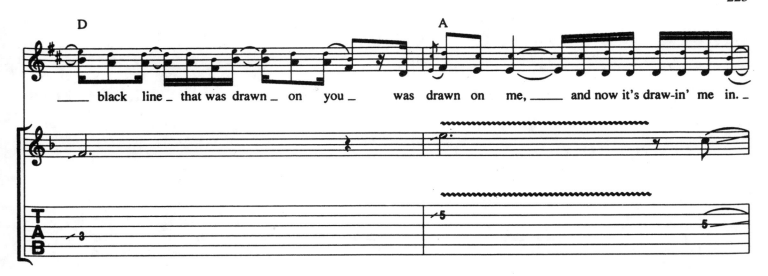

black line _ that was drawn _ on you _ was drawn on me, _ and now it's draw-in' me in. _

*Repeat and fade

Well, Sixth Av - e - nue heart - ache. _ Heart -
Sixth, Sixth Av - e - nue heart -

*All gtrs. ad lib. simile.

Verse 2:
Below me, there was a homeless man
Singing songs I knew complete.
On the steps alone, his guitar in hand.
His fifty years stood where he stands.
(To Chorus:)

Verse 3:
Walkin' home on those streets,
The river winds, they move my feet.
The subway steam, like silhouettes in dreams,
Stood by me, just like moonbeams.
(To Chorus:)

SO FAR AWAY

Elec. Gtrs. 1 & 2 tuned:
⑥ = A♭   ③ = D♭
⑤ = E♭   ② = E♭
④ = A♭   ① = A♭

Acous. Gtr. 1 & Elec. Gtr. 3 tuned down 1/2 step:
⑥ = E♭   ③ = G♭
⑤ = A♭   ② = B♭
④ = D♭   ① = E♭

Music by MICHAEL MUSHOK,
AARON LEWIS, JOHN APRIL
and JONATHAN WYSOCKI
Lyrics by AARON LEWIS

So Far Away - 6 - 1

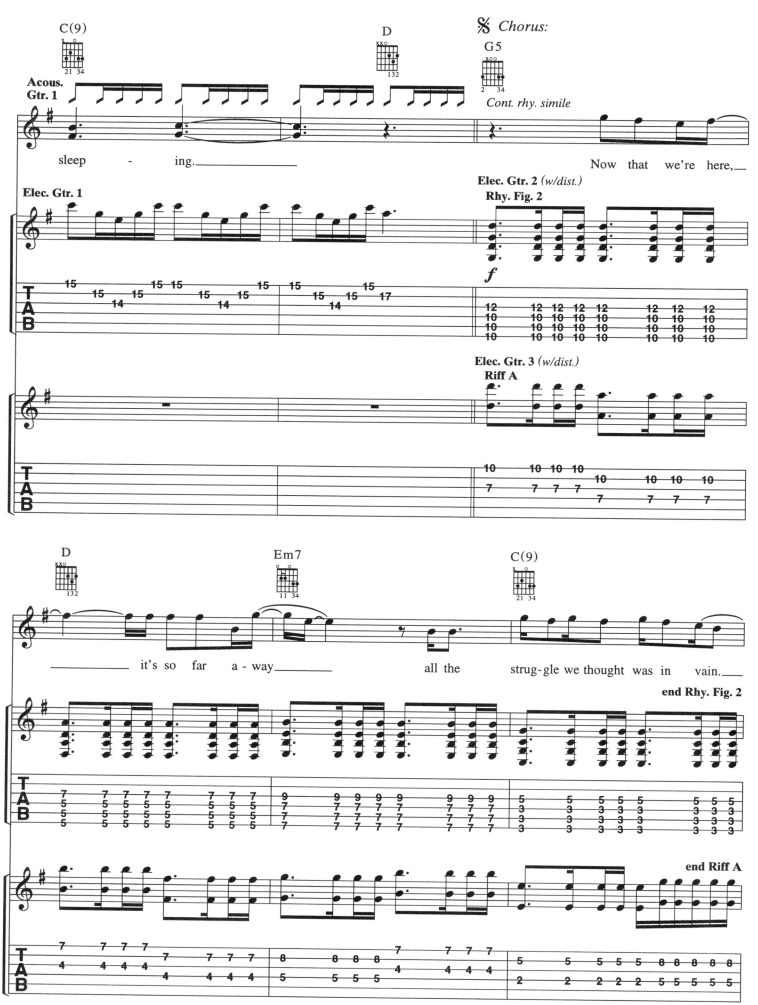

So Far Away - 6 - 4

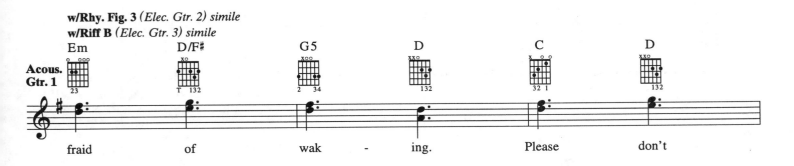

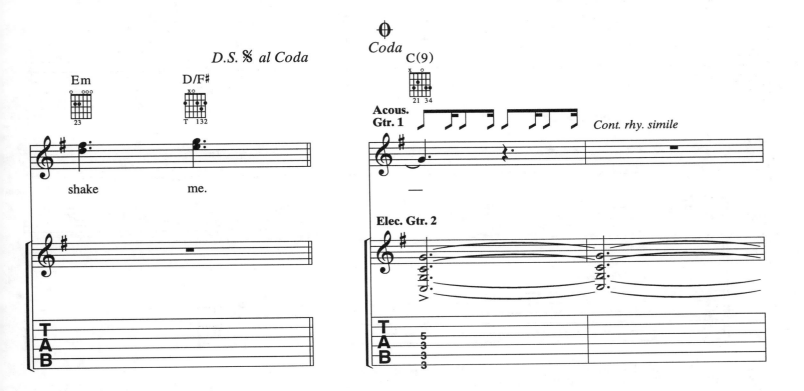

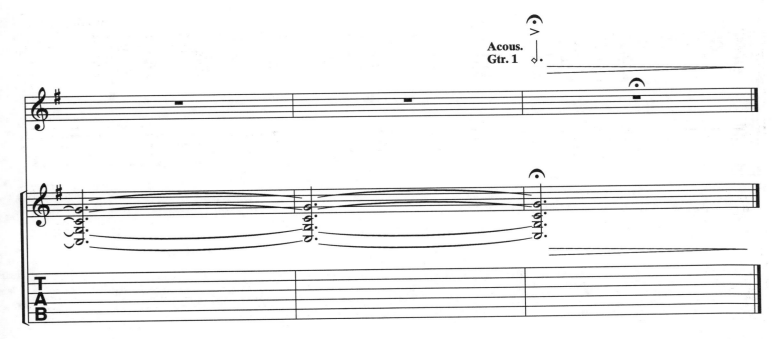

TIL I HEAR IT FROM YOU

Words and Music by
JESSE VALENZUELA, ROBIN WILSON
and MARSHALL CRENSHAW

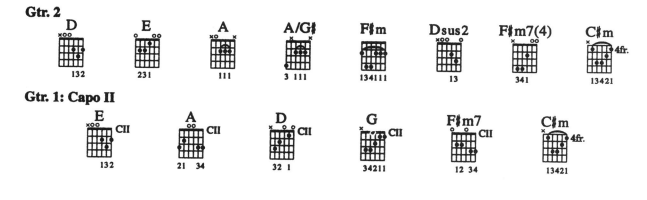

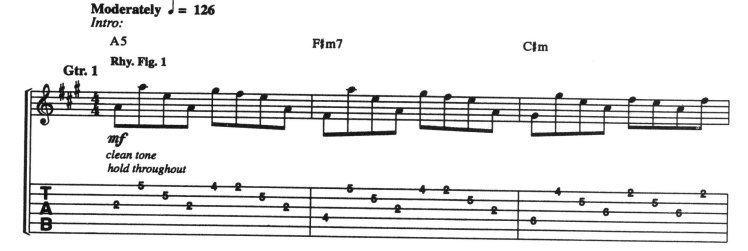

*Gtr. 1 w/capo at 2nd fret. TAB numbers indicate actual fret numbers with 2 thought of as open;
Gtr. 1 is two gtrs. arr. for one (throughout).

Til I Hear From You - 8 - 1

*Sing harmony 2nd time only.

Til I Hear From You - 8 - 2

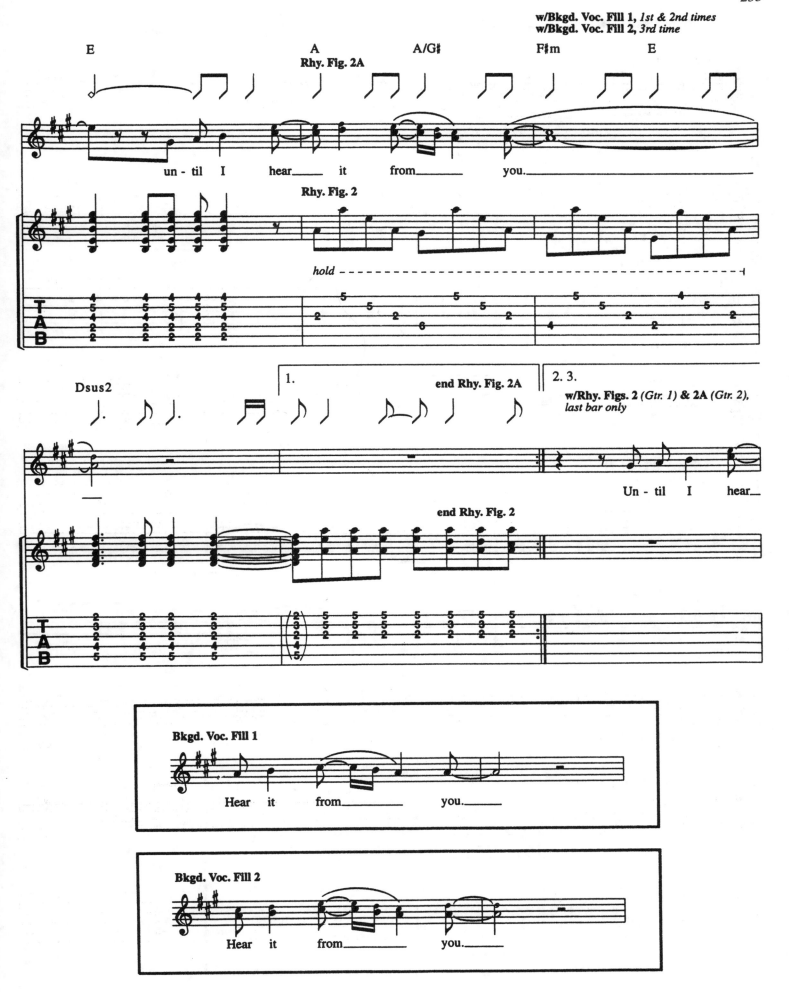

234

Til I Hear From You - 8 - 5

un - til I hear it from_____ you._____

236

Til I Hear From You - 8 - 7

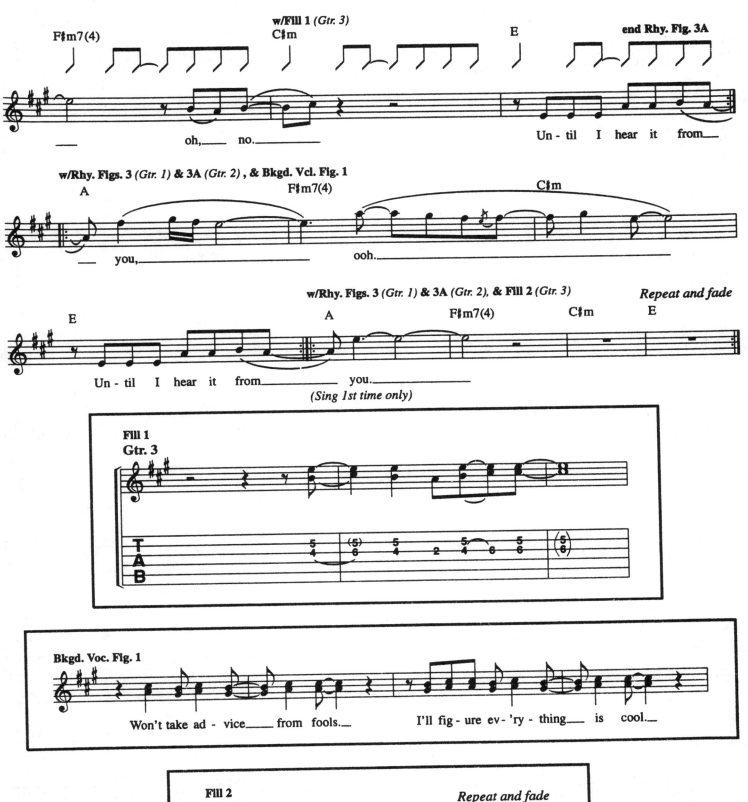

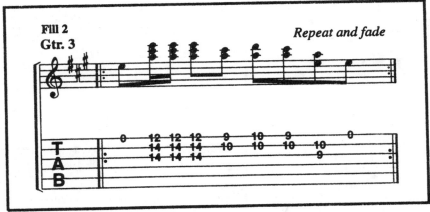

SMOOTH

Music and Lyrics by
ITAAL SHUR and ROB THOMAS

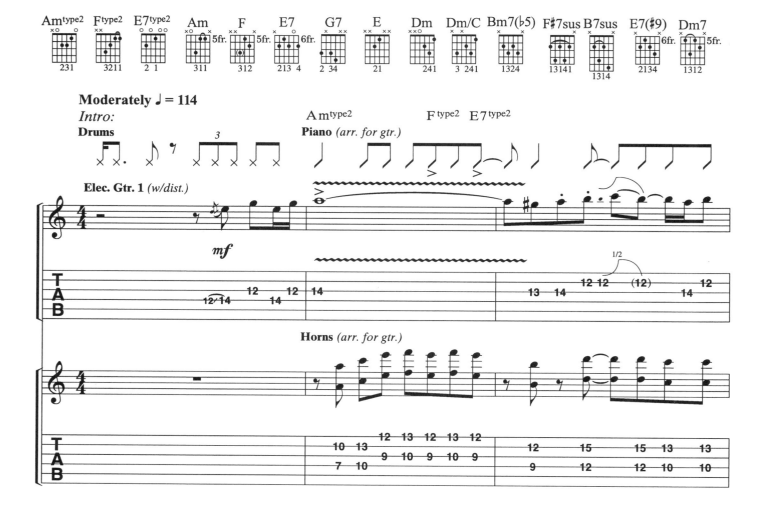

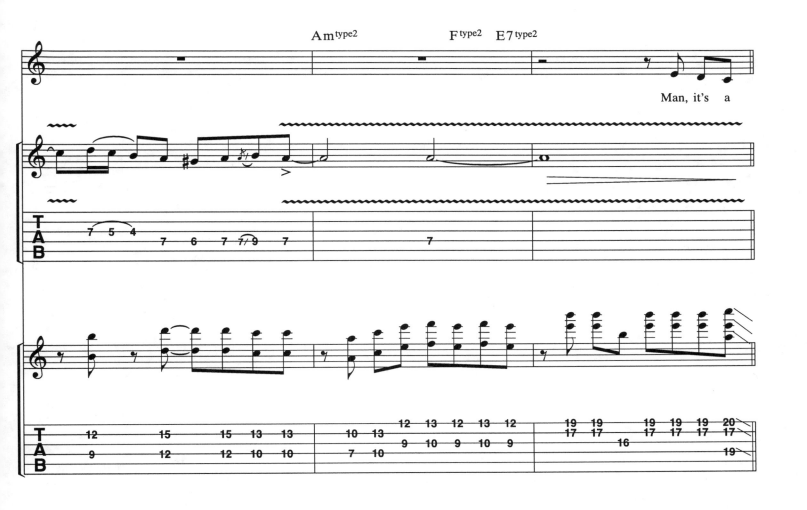

Verse 1:

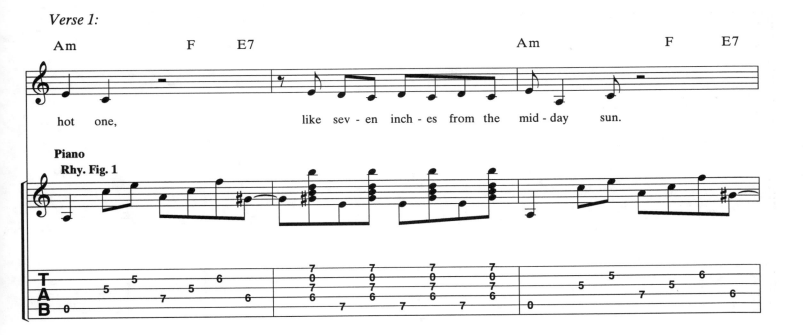

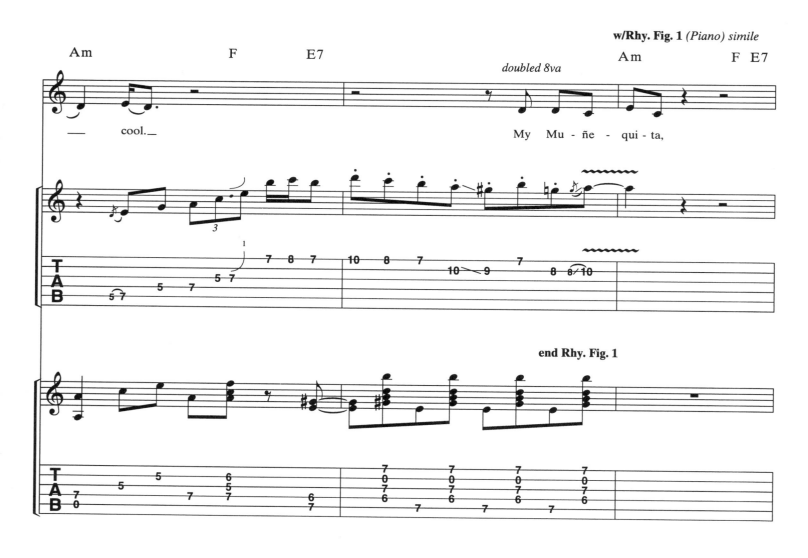

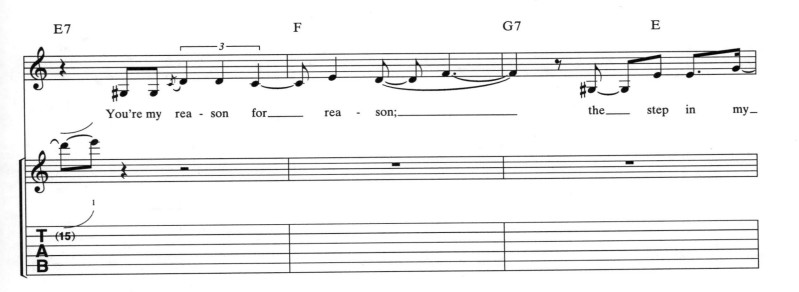

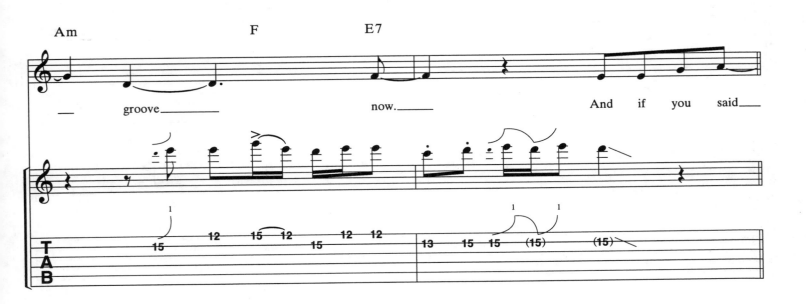

𝄋 *Pre-chorus:*

w/**Rhy. Fig. 2** *(Piano) 2 times, simile*

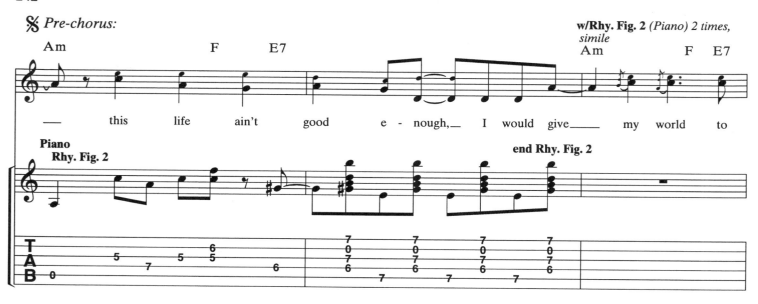

this life ain't good e- nough,__ I would give__ my world to

lift you up.__ I could change__ my life to bet- ter suit__ your__ mood.__

'Cause you're so__

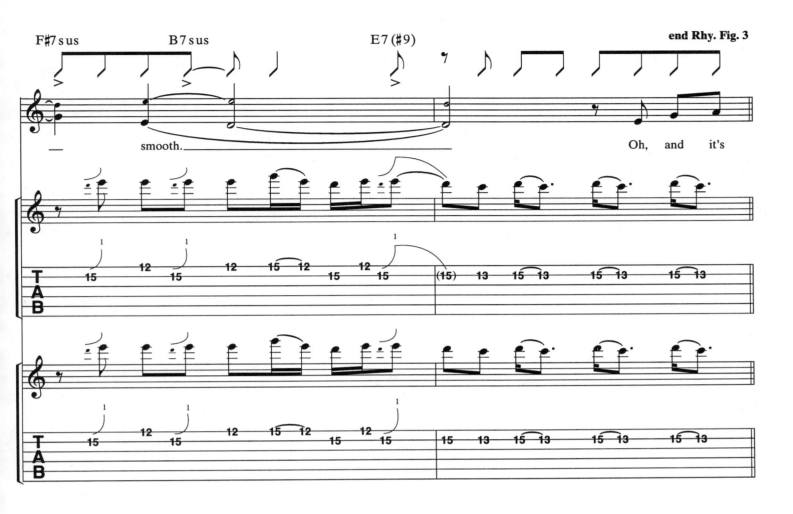

Chorus:
w/Rhy. Fig. 2 *(Piano) 3 times, simile*

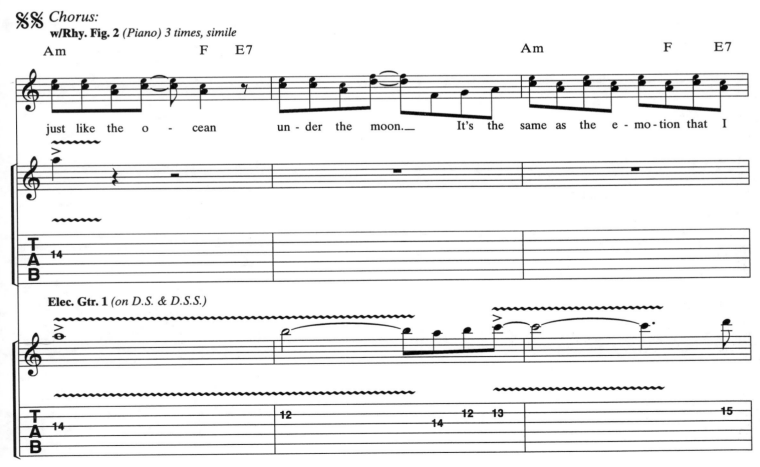

get from you.__ You got the kind of lov - ing that can be so smooth,__ yeah.

To Coda I
To Coda II
w//Rhy. Fig. 1 *(Piano) 1st 4 bars, simile*

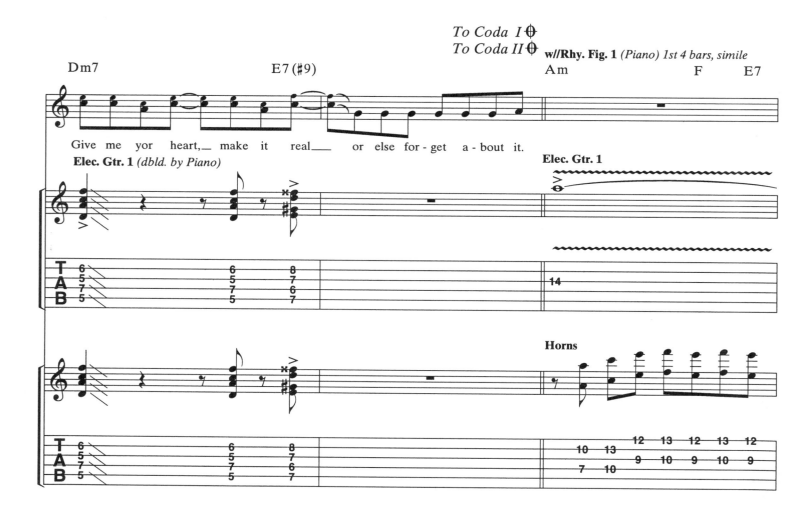

Give me yor heart,__ make it real___ or else for - get a - bout it.

Verse 2:
w/Rhy. Fig. 1 *(Piano) 2 times, simile*

Well, I'll tell you one thing if you would leave it be a cry-ing shame.__

In ev-'ry breath and ev-'ry word I hear your__ name call-ing me__

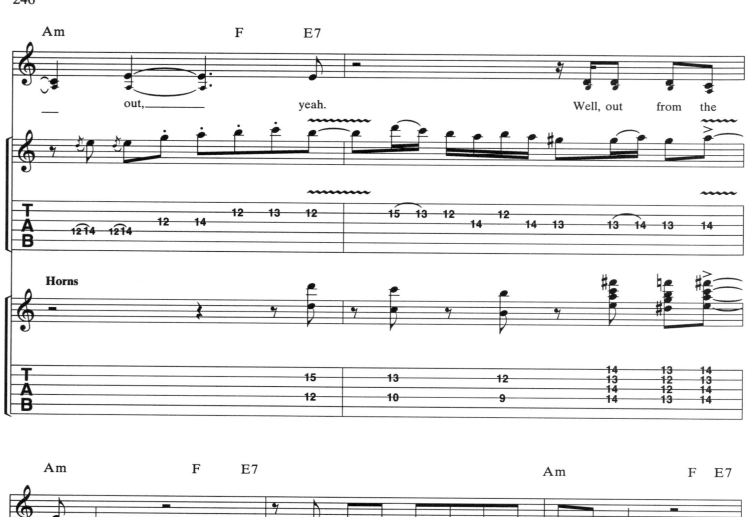

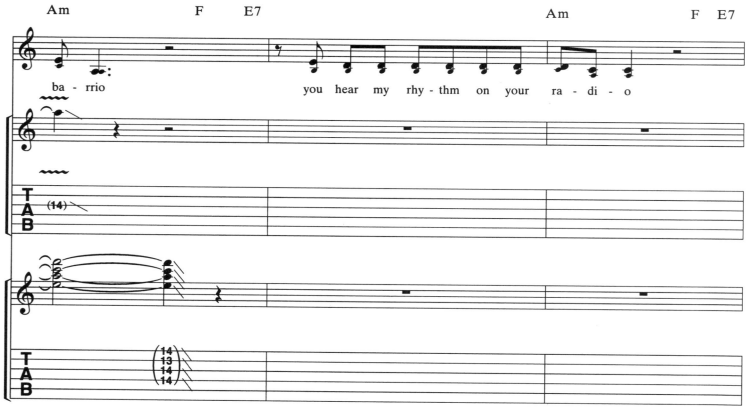

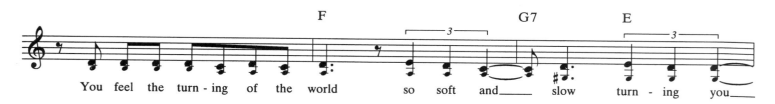

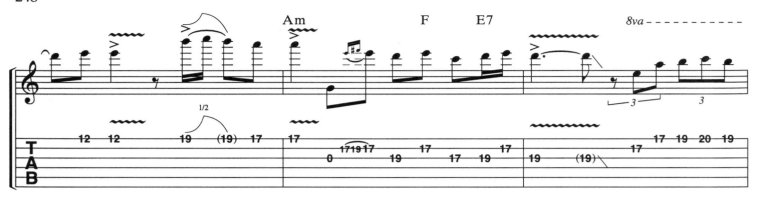

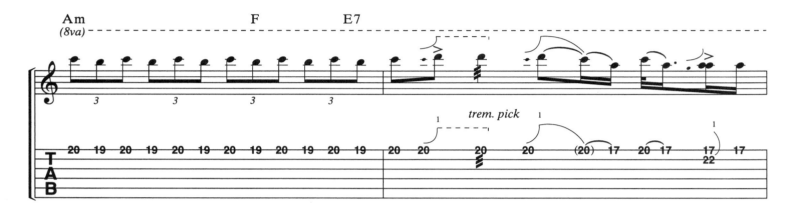

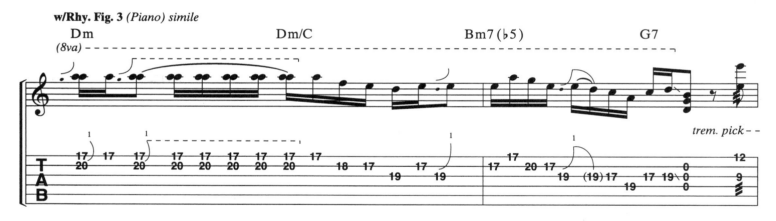

D.S.S. 𝄋𝄋 al Coda II

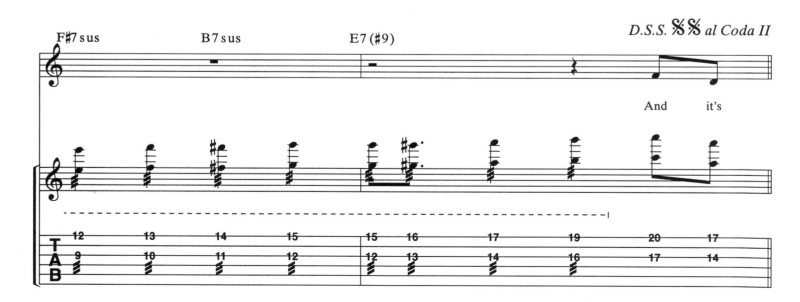

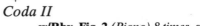

Coda II

w/Rhy. Fig. 2 *(Piano) 8 times, simile*

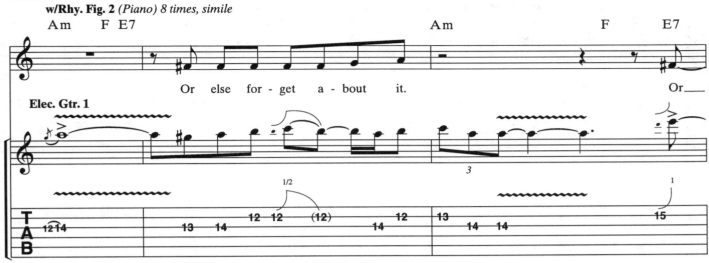

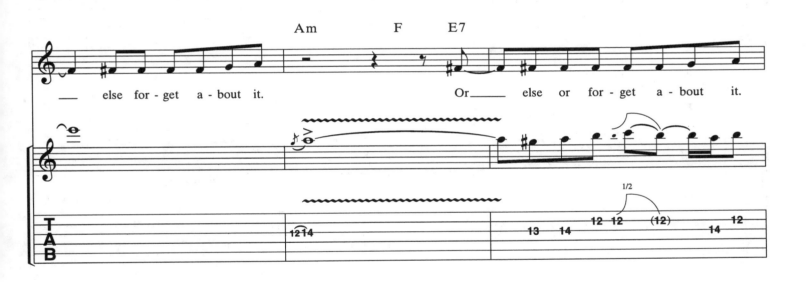

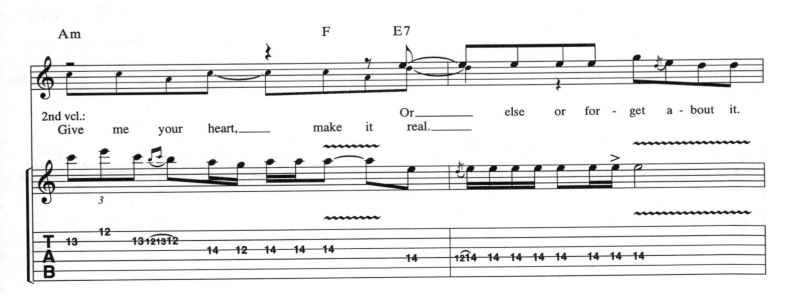

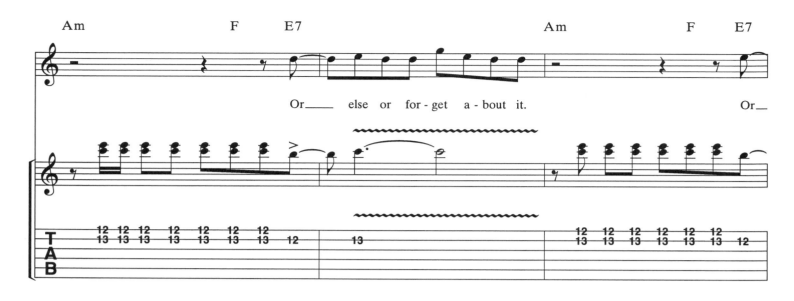

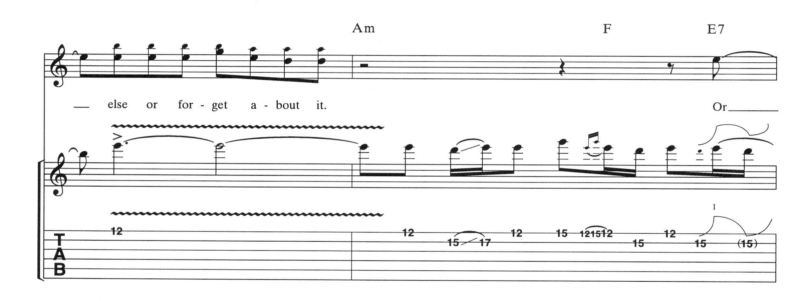

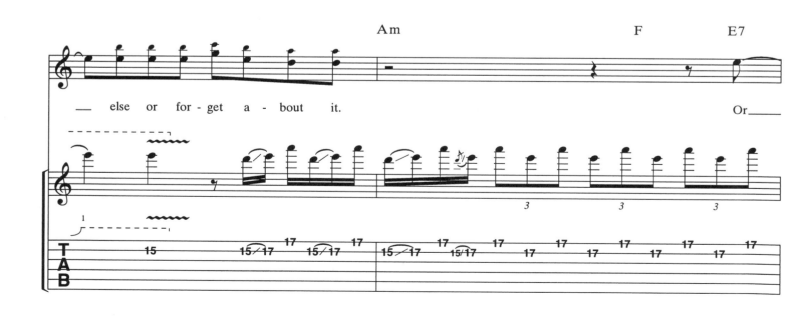

Slow Fade

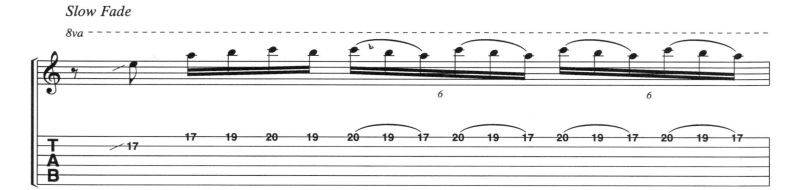

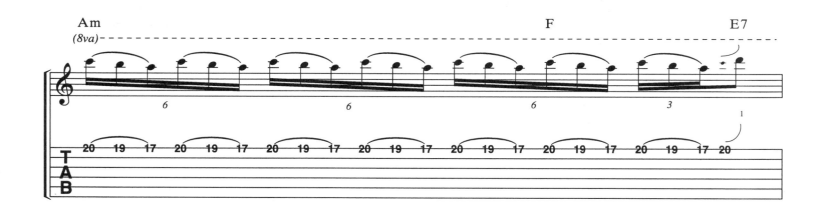

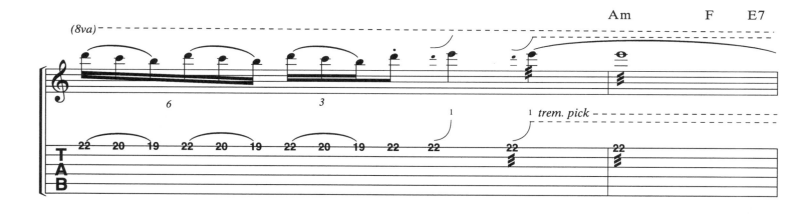

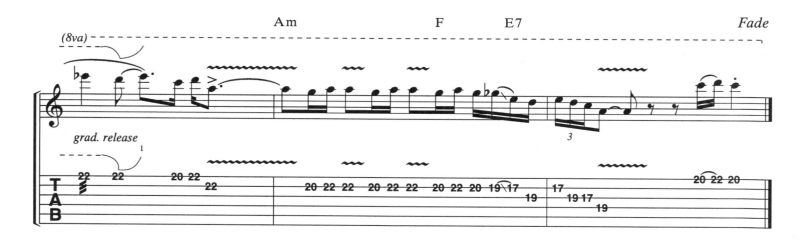

Someday

Lyrics by
CHAD KROEGER, MIKE KROEGER
and RYAN PEAKE
Music by
NICKELBACK

Someday - 5 - 3

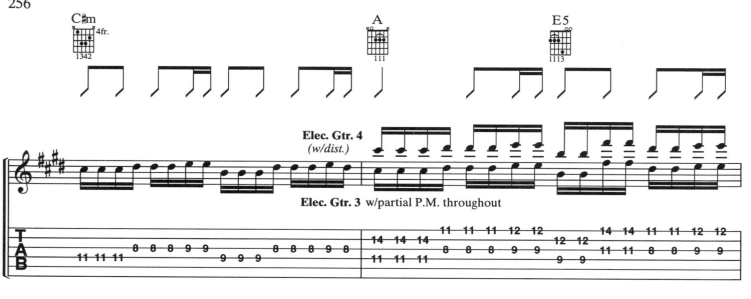

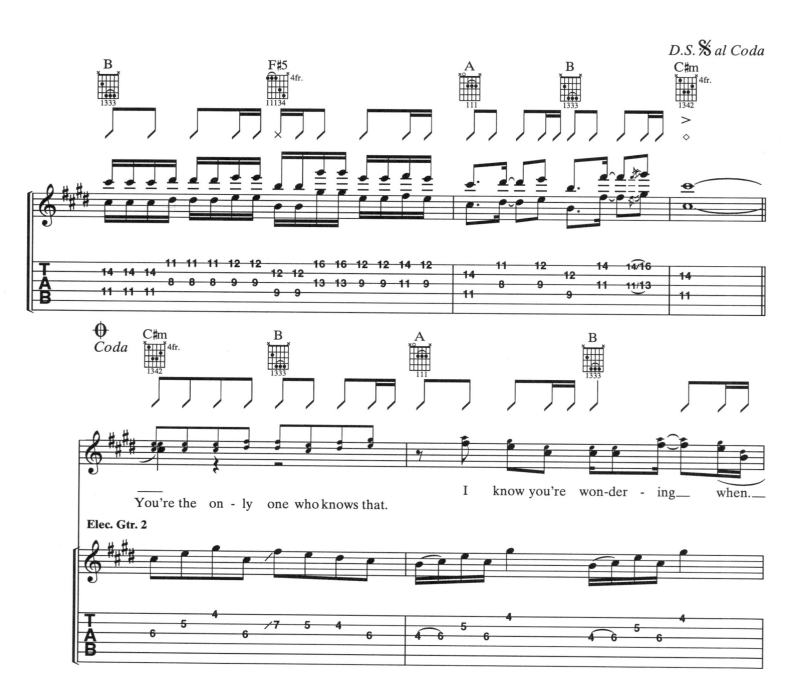

You're the on - ly one who knows that.

I know you're won-der-ing__ when.__

Elec. Gtr. 2

Verse 3:
How the hell did we wind up like this?
And why weren't we able to see the signs that we missed
And try to turn the tables?
Now the story's played out like this,
Just like a paperback novel.
Let's rewrite an ending that fits,
Instead of a Hollywood horror.
Nothing's wrong just as long as you know
That someday I will.
(To Chorus:)

WALKIN' ON THE SUN

Words and Music by
STEVE HARWELL, GREGORY CAMP,
PAUL DELISLE and KEVIN IANNELLO

Walkin' on the Sun - 8 - 1

Walkin' on the Sun - 8 - 2

260

Walkin' on the Sun - 8 - 3

Walkin' on the Sun - 8 - 4

265

WHEN I COME AROUND

Words by
BILLIE JOE

Music by
BILLIE JOE,
TRÉ COOL and MIKE DIRNT

When I Come Around - 3 - 1

Chorus:

Verse 2:
I heard it all before,
So don't knock down my door.
I'm a loser and a user so
I don't need no accuser
To try and slag me down, because I
Know you're right.
So go do what you like.
Make sure you do it wise.
You may find out that your
Self-doubt means nothing was ever there.
You can't go forcing something
If it's just not right.
(To Chorus:)